Creative Writing

Its role in evaluation

Margaret Wilkinson

King's Fund

Published by
King's Fund Publishing
11–13 Cavendish Square
London W1M 0AN

First published 1999

ISBN 1 85717 228 0

A CIP catalogue record for this book is available from the British Library

Available from:

King's Fund Bookshop
11–13 Cavendish Square
London W1M 0AN

Tel: 0171 307 2591
Fax: 0171 307 2801

Printed and bound in Great Britain

Contents

Contributors

Barbara Douglas is Whole Systems Co-ordinator, Newcastle Whole Systems, and can be contacted for further information c/o Newcastle Health City Project, 16 Great North Road, Newcastle NE2 4PS. Tel: 0191 233 0200

Angela Everitt is the local evaluator of the Whole Systems Initiative in Newcastle and North Tyneside and a member of the national evaluation team for the Urban Health Partnership. She has taught for 24 years at Middlesex University and the University of Northumbria and has published widely on practitioner research and evaluation. Her e-mail address is: angelaeveritt@readinglasses.demon.co.uk

Julian Pratt is a member of the Urban Health Partnership Group currently based at the King's Fund and can be contacted for further information at e-mail: wws@dial.pipex.com Tel: 0171 307 2675

Margaret Wilkinson teaches Creative Writing at the University of Northumbria. She is a novelist and former editor of the literary magazine, *Writing Women*.

Preface

WHOLE SYSTEMS THINKING is a series of working papers. They offer insights derived from putting ideas into practice as part of an action research programme – ideas about partnership and whole systems which are now central to the Government's ambitions for sustainable change, regeneration and the development of action zones in employment, education and health.

The papers reflect our experience of developing and applying a new approach to primary health care in cities. Similar issues of partnership and public participation arise elsewhere in the public sector and in the commercial world. We find much in common with people from many different organisations who recognise that, notwithstanding the new political climate, things are not really going to change if we just do 'more of the same'. They, and we, are looking for new ways of working.

WHOLE SYSTEMS THINKING is not a sequential series. It does not matter where you start from and none of the papers offers a complete picture. What we hope you find are thought-provoking ideas, particularly if you are curious about the kind of problems that return to haunt organisations over and over again. Some prove remarkably difficult to influence despite the best efforts of policy-makers and highly motivated people 'on the ground' – homelessness, for instance, and under-achievement in schools, long-term unemployment, 'sink' housing estates, family poverty. Issues like these need effective inter-agency work and consultation with the people who use the services, but even this can seem like a chore rather than part of the solution.

We have long experience of primary health care development in cities and a growing dissatisfaction with change initiatives which both fail to learn the lessons of earlier investment and to deliver desired outcomes. Four years ago we were in the position of developing a new action research programme whose focus was to be the intractable problems we refer to above. These may be recognised as 'wicked' problems. They are ill defined and constantly changing. They are perceived differently by different stakeholders and in trying to tackle them the tendency is to break them into actionable parts, which often turn into projects. We reasoned that if they could be recognised instead as issues for an interconnected system to tackle together, then they may become more tractable.

We chose to shift the focus of our work away from attention to parts and onto 'the whole' and thus to the connections between parts – how things fit together. This led us to explore ideas related to systems dynamics and the 'new science' of complexity. This has resulted in our designing a distinctive set of interventions which link ideas and practice and which we have called whole system working. This is a new development approach which does not offer certainty or guarantee success but it has rekindled our enthusiasm and that of many of the people with whom we are working.

We hope the ideas in these working papers enthuse you too. Because of our roots, many of the examples come from the health sector but we believe the concepts and the practical methods of working whole systems are widely applicable.

Pat Gordon, Diane Plamping, Julian Pratt
King's Fund

Whole Systems Thinking

The Urban Health Partnership is an action research programme on inter-agency working and public participation. The work is in London, Liverpool and Newcastle and North Tyneside, with health agencies and their local partners in housing, local government, commerce, police, transport, voluntary sector and local people.

Further information is available from:

Pat Gordon, Diane Plamping, Julian Pratt
Working Whole Systems
Urban Health Partnership
King's Fund
11–13 Cavendish Square
London W1M 0AN

Tel: +44(0)171 307 2675
Fax: +44(0)171 307 2801
e-mail: wws@dial.pipex.com
http://dialspace.dial.pipex.com/wws

PART 1

Creative writing and the whole systems approach in Newcastle and North Tyneside

Barbara Douglas

The Newcastle Health Partnership was formed to bring together the local authority, the health authority, the two universities and an umbrella voluntary sector organisation, recognising that improving the health of the population can be achieved only by working together. In 1995 the partnership chose to focus on older people and decided to adopt the 'whole systems' approach that was being developed by the Urban Health Partnerships team at the King's Fund (Pratt, Gordon & Plamping 1999).

This programme of work (Newcastle Whole Systems 1996, 1997, 1998) has allowed organisations to find new ways of working with each other, with citizens and with people who use their services. We hold meetings in different ways, whether large or small. Most of the work is done in conversations groups, often at round tables, and this holds true whether two or 200 people take part. We work through story-telling and narrative, which is initially frustrating for professionals until they begin to see the utility of this form of intelligence. There are no experts, or rather everyone is an expert. We work with the past, as well as the present and the future. We work in 'real time', not the usual committee mode. For many older people and front-line staff this is the first time they have had an opportunity to work on strategy or design alongside the 'high status' people. The work is about creating joint products which people care enough to work for, not a wish list for 'them' to deliver. People are encouraged to work with their own direct experience, rather than try to represent others. The work is about exploring possibilities before trying to find solutions to problems, and the methods are designed to make the common purpose explicit.

The programme has been evaluated by Angela Everitt (Everitt 1997, 1999) as part of the national evaluation programme led by Professor Jennie Popay (Popay et al. 1998). Evidence has been generated for the evaluation in three ways:

- semi-structured interviews
- direct observation
- encouraging participants to be self-evaluative.

Encouraging people to be self-evaluative was much more difficult than we expected. For a long time we tried to get people to spend the first few minutes of each meeting reflecting on what had happened since the last meeting; and the last minutes reflecting on the meeting itself. We found that people treated it as an unnecessary chore that got in the way of the work of the group.

After one particularly unsuccessful attempt we realised that perhaps group self-evaluation was never going to happen! Could we at least get people to be individually self-evaluative?

We knew that providing a pile of evaluation forms to be filled in at the end of each meeting would never get what we wanted. If this was to be congruent with the whole systems approach, it would not be a solitary activity and it would certainly be fun and creative. It would have to feed those involved. Perhaps we could help people to write creatively about their experiences . . .

Haiku

My first meeting meant
creatively writing and
all being honest

Remembering the present

I remember when the group met to do creative writing together. We had been a bit worried beforehand about how it would go. But on the day people who turned up really got into it, and some very useful material was produced.

I remember a discussion . . . at the creative writing session I focused on the work I was doing then . . . I decided to give more time to my own needs for leisure, pleasure and learning.

Poem

The time I have left
I will use to grow
flowers, fruit and leeks

In most people's work there is a tendency to focus on products and outcomes, leaving little time and space to reflect on the processes which made those outcomes possible. By using creative writing in the 'whole systems' evaluation process, participants have been able to reflect on, and perhaps understand for the first time, the way in which the 'whole systems' approach works, how it has influenced their daily practice and how it might be applied in the future. Examples have emerged which we might otherwise never have heard about.

During the creative writing workshops people have shared their experiences and understandings in ways which have brought greater cohesion to the group – reinforcing relationships and giving the group and individuals more confidence. Participants have been able to evaluate the 'whole systems' approach for themselves, as well as providing a wealth of material for the evaluation team. The process of creative writing has been fun, discovering new talents and the pleasure in writing itself, while enabling participants to reveal what they actually think about the approach in a candid, critical and constructive manner.

References

Everitt A (1997). *Urban Primary Care Initiative Newcastle 'Whole System Event': Interim evaluation report.* Salford: University of Salford

Everitt A (1999). *A Whole System Approach: Older people in Newcastle and North Tyneside*. Newcastle: Newcastle Whole Systems (in press)

Newcastle Whole Systems (1996, 1997, 1998). *Whole Systems Newsletters*. Newcastle: Newcastle Whole Systems

Popay J *et al.* (1998) *Urban Primary Health Care: Evaluating a 'whole systems' approach to development.* Salford: University of Salford (in press)

Pratt J, Gordon P & Plamping D (1999) *Working Whole Systems*. London: King's Fund (in press)

Why use creative writing?

Margaret Wilkinson

Creative writing is based on the premise that everyone has a story to tell and, with the right guidance, can tell it. Such stories can help describe social processes from the individual's point of view. The techniques suggested here will be new to both professionals and lay people. This has the effect of placing these two groups on a more equal footing when it comes to evaluation, problem-spotting and problem-solving.

Creative writing techniques value each and every story that is told, each and every viewpoint that is expressed. Group processes thereby become more democratic as each person is under the same constraint and each viewpoint carries equal weight. The results can provide a series of pictures describing how it feels for different people to be part of the social processes under scrutiny. The ideas that emerge – not only from the writing but from the interactions stimulated by the workshops – will reveal layers of truth, often contradictory, from multiple viewpoints. This subjectivity allows an evaluator to build up a picture of the impact of such processes, and services, on individuals.

The teaching of creative writing has developed in many ways over the last ten years. As an academic subject, it now commands a place on undergraduate English courses as well as being a postgraduate subject in its own right. It has been offered as part of return-to-learning courses, access courses, community projects and group therapy. It has been used in a wide variety of settings and with many different student groups, including primary school children, prisoners, people with a terminal illness, people with learning disabilities, drug users, people with low levels of educational achievement as well as university students. While I was leading workshops for the Whole Systems Initiative in Newcastle-upon-Tyne I realised that creative writing could provide a powerful tool in qualitative evaluation, as well as enhancing group operations and cohesion, highlighting problems and offering possible solutions.

The exercises in this workbook are based on writing games and improvisational writing techniques, and on storytelling and memory. They are uniquely empowering, affirming, problem-solving and democratising. Writing games and improvisational writing allow people to make discoveries as they write, to access ideas they may not have known they had, find hidden connections, juxtapose concepts, break down familiar boundaries in their thinking, make accidents happen, think with their pens and generally see the act of writing as producing insights. Order often emerges from accident, free-thinking and improvisation.

The storytelling exercises affirm and shape individual voices and seek relevant links between past experience and current change. They make use of history to describe the future and hearing these stories aloud validates and shares individual realities.

Creative writing techniques tease out information that might be difficult to obtain by other means, emotionally truthful responses, for example. By concentrating on the strict rules and instructions that accompany these exercises or on juggling language, form and imagery, people often find themselves taking more risks with the content of what they are writing. Unusual starting points, quirky exercises and uncertainty about where the exercises are leading mean that people approach the whole experience in a new way, without controlling the outcome.

When social enterprises are being evaluated, people are frequently asked to comment on content and meaning, and the results can be disappointingly unsurprising and formulaic. When using writing exercises, however, syllabic counting or prescribed vocabulary or repetition rules seem just as important as content or meaning. The resulting responses are often fresher, less censored, almost unconsciously produced because evaluation is not dictated by familiar evaluative jargon and processes. Evaluation seems, instead, to become a by-product of creative thinking.

Writing itself is a source of satisfaction: experiential, educational and craft-based. Demystifying the process of writing, via the exercises, is an enjoyable and empowering feeling. In addition to other surprising outcomes, all the participants will almost certainly leave the workshop having written a poem or shaped a piece of prose.

What happens in a creative writing session? Short exercises are set. These are done by the group, on the spot, in a limited amount of time. Responses are read out loud. People are asked to listen and there is time for discussion.

Why write on the spot? Because people can make discoveries even when they think they know how they feel about a certain issue. Limited time, group pressure and unusual exercises are all important factors in helping people encounter an idea from a different perspective and write about it subjectively. Why read out what you have written? Because everyone gets the opportunity to hear their own words read in their own voice. This often provides powerful individual and collective experience. Why listen to others read aloud? Because the trust established by agreeing to read to each other and agreeing to listen carefully to each other is an important part of the group process. The pieces read aloud can inspire, question, spark disagreement, redefine issues and encourage conversation. Finally, there is an opportunity for questions, commentary, feedback and discussion and the group's response to the exercise as a whole. Feedback will usually be about the issues and emotions raised rather than the technique and craft of writing but, whether the group facilitator is a writer or not, some response about the ability of writing to clarify, move and focus can almost always be given.

The nature of the exercises in this book is elastic. The tasks can be easy or challenging. They can be used singly or in a developmental way to build up patterns. They can be tailored to meet the needs of specific groups of people and to address specific evaluation purposes. Not only are the results satisfying and even surprising but creative writing can be fun as well as producing ideas and insights.

Writing creatively for evaluation

Angela Everitt and Julian Pratt

Creative writing for evaluation is based on a particular understanding of the dynamic relationships between generating evidence and making judgements: and between evaluation (evidence and judgement) and action.

Evaluation is different from research. Research is to do with finding out; evaluation is to do with making value judgements informed by research. Evidence generated through research can, and should, inform evaluative judgements but evidence does not dictate these judgements. Evaluation has been understood as comprising two separate, but interrelated, components: that to do with generating evidence; and that to do with making judgements (Everitt & Hardiker 1996). These two components can be separated conceptually and it is useful to do so in order to ensure that both are given due attention. In practice, however, the two are intertwined.

We set out below our analytical thinking about the relationship between evidence, judgement and action. We conceptualise these as distinct entities in order to alert us to different processes at work in programme evaluation. However, the essence of our approach is to understand the interconnectedness of evidence, judgement and action. The dichotomising of evaluation and policy is rejected in favour of an approach that recognises the making of policy through practices.

The developmental story of evaluation

Before pursuing our approach to evaluation in more detail, it may be helpful to locate it in the recent developmental story of evaluation. Evaluation, as part of the repertoire of new public-sector management approaches of the 1980s and 1990s, adopted a technical approach imbued with ways of knowing about the world broadly informed by logical positivism. Evaluation became a requirement of public funding: outputs and outcomes had to be decided at the outset and the extent to which these were achieved was to be measured quantitatively. This approach assumed that measures could be refined to be objective, and evaluation was conceived as separate from ongoing practice. Evaluation findings, the measurements, were intended to inform policy and resource allocation decisions in a rational, linear way. Policy analysts have pointed out that one significant effect of this approach to evaluation was to control devolved and increasingly fragmented practices (Gray & Jenkins 1993).

Alternative approaches to research and evaluation have placed more emphasis on subjective ways of knowing. Pluralistic approaches to evaluation have valued the multiple perspectives of professional practitioners, managers and lay people (including citizens and people who use services) – all those involved in initiatives being evaluated (Smith & Cantley 1985). In pluralistic studies, perspectives that are possibly competing or conflicting are set down in evaluation reports. With the report in the hands of the commissioner of the evaluation, or the manager to whom the evaluation is addressed, implicitly it is left to them to decide which views to take into account when making resource and policy decisions.

In their Fourth Generation evaluation approach, Guba & Lincoln (1989) highlighted the problem of power in evaluation. They revealed ways in which power shaped both people's views and the processes through which those views are articulated. They argued that, in the context of multiple views, evaluators had responsibilities to intervene in evaluative processes in order to facilitate debate between different actors. They left it with the evaluators, not the managers or commissioners, to reach evaluative conclusions.

New ways of thinking about knowledge have revealed the ways in which research produces many truths rather than the truth (Barrett 1991). Everitt & Hardiker (1996) have developed an approach to evaluation that takes account of this post-modern world. Here, the evaluator is concerned with revealing the many truths of practice, and with having regard for the powerful ways in which some views come to be regarded as the truth. The role of the evaluator becomes concerned with facilitating processes to deconstruct what has come to be thought of as 'true', while at the same time providing opportunities for alternative discourses to be articulated. Recognising evidence as producing many truths makes the place of judgement-making in evaluation central. Dialogue and debate are fostered to articulate different truths but also to engage in judgement-making.

Our approach to evaluation

In the process of evaluating the 'whole systems' work in Newcastle it has seemed appropriate to develop an approach to evaluation that is consistent with the whole systems approach itself. Whole systems working enables organisations and networks of organisations to explore and create their future together (Pratt, Gordon & Plamping 1999). Participants, including lay people and people working in organisations at strategic, monitoring and operational levels, contribute many different perspectives. They work with their personal experiences and bring together the traditionally separate activities of research, analysis, decision-making, implementation and review into a single process. An evaluation approach consistent with this necessarily emphasises participation in the integration of evaluation and action.

We now give attention in turn to the three aspects of our approach to evaluation: generating evidence, making value judgements, and integrating evaluation with action.

Generating evidence

During the 'whole systems' work in Newcastle groups ranging from two to 200 people, from a variety of different backgrounds, met to explore how they could do something about a range of issues they cared passionately about. Some of the smaller groups, of 10–20 people, who had been meeting regularly accepted the offer of creative writing workshop to explore their experiences of whole systems working. The examples that follow were written during these workshops and have contributed to the evaluation of the whole systems work in Newcastle.

Most research traditions emphasise the gathering of ideas and data, things of the mind. Co-operative Inquiry (Reason 1994) identifies, in addition to this 'propositional' knowledge, three other aspects of knowledge: experiential, practical and presentational. In our evaluative approach we seek to engage with all of these four types of knowledge. People articulate their experiences of a programme or project in many kinds of ways. In order to engage with the four types of knowledge, we need to think imaginatively about the most appropriate ways for different people: for example, drawing pictures and taking photographs may be particularly appropriate for children; forum theatre has been imaginatively used by disadvantaged people and disabled people (Boal 1993). Creative writing can be engaging, and enjoyable, for professionals and lay people alike.

Experiential knowledge

Experiential knowing means direct encounter, face-to-face meeting. It is knowing through participative, empathic resonance with a being, so that as knower I feel attuned with it and distinct from it.

Experiential knowing cannot be accessed directly through those methods of enquiry that strive to maintain distance and objectivity. Knowing our experiences requires that we have some direct conduit into self, into our personal. Researchers who focus on exploring subjectivities, albeit through recognising the inter-subjectivity of researcher–researched relations, are able to reveal subjective knowing. These researchers abandon predetermined sets of questions in favour of conversations with those researched, perhaps guided by interview schedules. Creative writing is a way of generating evidence which enables people to access this inner knowing without having to respond to questions imposed upon them by outside researchers.

Three ways I see myself differently at whole systems meetings compared with other meetings

I feel as though I am among friends
I can be open, explore ideas, take risks, have a laugh and some fun
What matters is the real purpose of what we are trying to achieve, not kudos or benefit for one organisation or individual – trying at least to lose the hidden agendas

I am among friends
I can be open, take risks
The purpose matters

Ways in which experiences of whole systems meetings had affected other aspects of my life

I say hello to new people in the supermarket
I take learning into my everyday world

Using the whole system approach

Without order and control, people didn't interrupt each other. There must have been twelve people there – all women. We sat quite formally around a rectangular table. At first I felt quite frustrated as I often do at the beginning of meetings. Why had this meeting not been planned? Why were there no papers sent out before the meeting for us to read and prepare ourselves? I still feel confused. The contradiction between on the one hand people shouldn't waste the time of others by speaking off the top of their heads. We owe it to others to speak in an informed way and yet, and yet? The meeting showed the value of people engaging personally together talking about matters that would not have been agenda'd. Everyone had a say, everyone stayed. There was no difference between asking questions, raising problems, speaking tentatively, and proposing possible things to try. Possible ways forward. No one had only the answers. Everyone had questions and vulnerabilities as well as answers and autonomy. Spontaneous democracy. How? We have been talking about values and purpose in ways that are so strange, ways usually excluded from us. How often do we talk like this within organisations? We are not allowed to.

Propositional knowledge

Propositional knowing is knowing in conceptual terms; knowledge by description. This kind of knowing is expressed in statements, theories and formulae that come with the mastery of concepts and classes that language bestows.

Sometimes the opportunity for creative writing brings statements and theories to the surface. Perhaps these could have been accessed by a more formal and directed approach, but the creative writing may enable people to be more reflective and to include contradictory views as well as describing other aspects of knowledge along with the proposistional.

Using the whole system approach

The 'saneness' of the discussion came as a surprise. People talked about things they really value and feel strongly about. They then tried to relate these 'real things' to the way in which they worked or their organisations work. It opened up new horizons, new visions, new possibilities. It was exciting and stimulating and felt very 'real'. Drawing back from the excitement and the wealth of possibility is hard and frightening. How can we make it happen? What stops us making some of these things a reality? How do we get there? The ways forward often seem 'quirky' and different, but it's hard to fight against falling back into the way an organisation has always done things or how we can make it fit into existing structures. There comes a stage when you simply want to hand it all over to someone to 'do' but the 'real' solutions don't work like that. You have to keep working on it together. It usually involves a bit more effort, a few more connections, more people to persuade and cajole into looking at things differently. It's tough and it's often confusing.

Using the whole systems approach

EXCITED

The possibilities of a whole range of organisations pulling together to meet the same end whereas they might normally be working in isolation on a small section of the population, when organisations work together the relationships formed spill over into many of the sub-groups you are involved with and good friendships can be developed. This excites me!!

SURPRISED
By the range of organisations that were involved in the event and the range of members, i.e. from health/directors to volunteers. They all want to share the same vision so it begs the question why it is so difficult to achieve. This doesn't surprise me but the fact that people want it but don't achieve it does.

FRIGHTENED
By the theories that are used and whether I would be able to adapt these to my everyday work. The concept of open space technology is all very well but what happens if the main issue for discussion is left untouched? At times I feel out of my depth but this could be down to not having a good initial understanding of the whole systems concept.

COURAGE
Would be required to speak up, questioning theories and concepts being promoted and pointing out limitations to the model. People seem very taken by the approach and perhaps it needs/begs to be questioned as to its effective use of time or is it high-falutin bull-shit! I'm undecided.

DIFFERENT
From any approaches I have come across although in saying that I feel that concepts have been given names which describe something that already exists. The difference with this approach is that everybody seems committed to trying to make it succeed. If it does that . . .

Four thing's I've got from this group

Taken away the feelings of isolation
Motivated, and moved forward
Provided me with new information, possibilities, ideas and knowledge
Made me appreciate the ways people can work together in a variety of ways

People sitting at individual tables with cappuccinos – like a café
Offers of help in carrying out a possibly difficult task
Laughter ideas and creativity
People exploring imaginative ways of working together

Practical knowledge

Practical knowing is knowing how to do something, demonstrated in a skill or competence. It brings knowing to fruition in purposive deeds, and consummates them with its autonomous celebration of excellent accomplishment.

Capturing this practical knowing is difficult. However, when people reflect on their experiences of a programme or project through writing creatively about them, they can reveal to others and themselves ways in which they have become skilled and competent and made contributions to action – as the following examples indicate.

Using the whole system approach myself

Deciding to use self-organising groups. This felt like a big risk for lots of things. Personally – that people would think that I wasn't doing my job properly; that people would think that their time was wasted; that people would run out of things to say before the end of the workshop; that people would not 'play' or use it. Typing out the procedure for running self-organising groups and going through it, using the mike so that everyone knew what to do next – and then going and sitting down and letting the people at the workshop get on with it. The silence began slowly to be filled as people began taking charge of their groups and didn't walk out.

Sticking to the decision to use self-organising groups at the disastrous beginning when the room had not been laid out properly and the speaker to introduce the paper did not arrive – and it worked, people used it, were glad they'd gone and said they'd learned a lot. People were in themed tables, arranged to avoid any major personality clashes. Would it work if that was not done or should tables be allocated?

My question now though is how to use this practice of organising participation in meetings to make purposeful change, and still get everyone to join in with the approach.

How can we make it more routine to discuss issues/problems and arrive at change through participation? How can the action group I convene use the approach more?

The march

One woman said, 'I've never done anything like this before – do you think we'll be on telly tonight?' It reminded me of the demos of my twenties . . . for many of them it was a new and exciting experience. We marched down Northumberland Street with the brass band playing at the front – some people singing and linking arms as went. That sense of the strength of a large group of people with a common purpose – probably not a frequent feeling for many of the older people who had come along – we felt strong (the police had moved people out of the way as we marched along). This was an afternoon for fun and making Newcastle aware that older people need to be seen and don't sit at home knitting with the cat.

Remembering

I remember a group event for the over 50s in June 1997. The start of many cycling days developing skills health and fun. I remember Dec 1997 still going rain or cold there's no stopping the people who have matured not grown old.

I remember older people becoming teachers of keep fit for others. Viewing their session with delight getting a buzz out of what they had done and I might.

I remember a feeling of pride. Seeing the older people perform in front of Tyne Tees cameras. The training course had done wonders for their self-esteem and the group had initiated and made this possible.

Presentational knowledge

Presentational knowing clothes our encounter with the world in the metaphors of aesthetic creation. It draws on expressive and symbolic forms of imagery. It symbolises both our felt attunement with the world and the primary meaning which it holds for us.

Creative writing is one approach to 'presentational' knowing which can be readily heard by others and is durable for further re-readings and interpretations as evidence is taken into judgement-making and action.

Using the language of a newspaper cutting to describe the whole systems approach

In general, working with other agencies can often be a volatile business which descends into the brown sulphurous dirt of competitiveness and misunderstanding. Meetings can seem like a crowd of people gathering in a pungent dark crypt trying to decipher the Egyptian hieroglyphics that represent our individual cultures. The whole systems approach, however, has more clarity and colour. Its strength is the sharing and developing understanding of common nutty problems, indeed the drawing out and making visible the amino acids that bind our work together.

Imagining my childhood hero/heroine attending a whole systems meeting

Mr Kinmond was a very intelligent, sporting and energetic teacher who simply loved people and who oozed confidence. If he was at the whole systems event I can visualise him enthusiastically writing and at the same time speaking his ideas at the blackboard (or flipchart). He would also be in his element moving from group to group to encourage people and give advice on idea development and promote initiative.

Hayley Mills comes in, smartly dressed, full of confidence. She greets everyone like old friends. She seems to need to have a quick chat with a few different people, fixing up meetings or sorting something out. Hayley always seems to have a finger in so many pies. Throughout the meeting Hayley always seems to have a pertinent point to make – she has so many good connections; she knows the right people to talk to, she's in a position to influence things. We're always pleased when Hayley can make the meeting. It's not quite the same without her. She's fun too – there's always a good anecdote, so we have a laugh and a bit of fun – event though it's a serious business.

Making value judgements

Creative, artistic and personal ways of generating evidence, in contrast to, say, the self-completion of semi-structured questionnaires, highlight the ways in which evidence and judgement are, in practice, integrated. When people write or act in passionate ways about their experiences, they draw upon their own evidence but also imbue this with their value judgements. At this personal level, evidence and judgement are inseparable.

Technical approaches to evaluation assume that the data, the measurements of outputs and outcomes, reveal the truth and that there is no need for judgement-making. Pluralist approaches reveal multiple perspectives, the many truths of practice, but leave the evaluation judgements with the commissioner, manager or the evaluator. Our approach here is to explore ways of placing the appraisal of evidence and the making of these judgements firmly with all those engaged in the practices. This expands the responsibility for the evaluation and action to include lay people and practitioners as well as managers and evaluators, both across and within organisations. Stories and images are shared and debated, differences between articulated experiences acknowledged. People engage in processes to seek to understand and to explain how it is that they experience practices differently and how it is that they make different evaluative judgements. Importantly, people question what has come to be thought of as true and opportunities are made and grasped for alternative stories to be told and heard.

Evaluation and action

In both pluralistic and fourth generation approaches, the evaluator produces written reports to be fed into the policy arenas. The relationship between the findings in the evaluation report and the action subsequently taken, informed by these findings, is assumed to be linear and rational (Bulmer 1984). Our approach recognises evidence, judgement and action as three vital components of evaluations which interact simultaneously. This approach to evaluation adopts a different understanding of the relationship between 'finished' evaluation studies and policy decisions informed by them. In our model, evaluation is emphasised as process rather than product, evaluations are never 'finished' but are essential processes if organisations are to be open to critical questioning and learning. Thus, rather than the policy arenas being the depository of evaluation reports, policy is understood as produced through the myriad of practices that take place in and between organisations and their users. Policies experienced are those produced through multiple practices. Engaging in evaluative talk about ways in which these practices are experienced, countering what may have become known in organisations as 'the' truth of these practices and telling alternative stories has the effect of changing practices in dynamic and ongoing ways (Fraser 1989). The practice of evaluation, of generating evidence and making judgements is also about the practice of ever-changing practices and policies.

Through the experience of whole systems working, we discovered ways in which conversations trigger actions. These took place between programme participants – managers and practitioners, across and within organisations, and lay people. Likewise, evaluative conversations took place, not just between the evaluator and the programme participants, but among all participants. Change arising through these conversations develops organically as talk shapes understandings and interventions.

We are developing ways in which the outputs of creative writing workshops may serve a narrative role in written reports and participatory events similar to the role of conversations in whole systems ways of working.

References

Barrett M (1991). *The Politics of Truth: From Marx to Foucault*. Cambridge: Polity Press.

Boal A (1993). *Theatre of the Oppressed*. London: Pluto Classics.

Bulmer M (1984). *The Uses of Social Research: Social investigation in public policy-making*. London: Allen and Unwin

Everitt A & Hardiker P (1996). *Evaluating for Good Practice*. Basingstoke: Macmillan

Fraser N (1989). Talking about needs: interpretative contests as political conflicts in welfare state societies. *Ethics* 99, January: 291–313

Gray A & Jenkins B (1993). Markets, managers and the public service: the changing of a culture. In: Taylor-Gooby P & Lawson R (eds). *Markets and Managers: New issues in the delivery of welfare*. Buckingham: Open University Press

Guba EG & Lincoln YS (1989). *Fourth Generation Evaluation*. Newbury Park (CA) and London: Sage Publications

Pratt J, Gordon P & Plamping D (1999). *Working Whole Systems*. London: King's Fund

Reason (1994). Three approaches to participative inquiry. In: Denzin NK & Lincoln YS (eds). *Handbook of Qualitative Research*. Thousand Oaks: Sage

Smith G & Cantley C (1985). *Assessing Health Care: A study in organisational evaluation*. Milton Keynes: Open University Press.

Section 1

Easy

Exercise 1

Object riddle

Purpose

This is a good first exercise, or ice-breaker, because it provides an offbeat way of introducing group members to each other – using alternative identities. It is also an affirming exercise that builds self-confidence in writing by producing something similar to a real poem immediately, and thus helps demystify the process of writing from the beginning of the workshop.

Method

Prepare an envelope full of strips of paper on which you have written the names of ordinary objects – simple, concrete objects seem to work better. The ones I use include: **a cup; an egg; a chair; ink; a newspaper; a shoe; a pillow; a cigarette**. In the workshop pass the envelope around and let participants blindly choose a strip of paper. Each participant must become the object written on their strip of paper. ('You are the object you've picked.') Writing in first person ('I am'), participants describe themselves in four to seven sentences, without mentioning the name of the object. They try to fool the group, but they must be truthful. Then the riddles are read out, and group members try to guess the object's identity.

Remind participants how traditional riddles are written. In a traditional 'What am I?' riddle, the hidden object is described by both what it is like (what it resembles), and what it is not like. What it does, and what it cannot do. Participants might want to vary the beginning of their sentences, so that each sentence doesn't always start with the pronoun I.

10 minutes' writing time.

Variations

The object names in the envelope can be tailored to address group needs and specific issues. For example, at a workshop exploring conventional views of old age, some of the object names in the envelope included: **a photo album; a bus pass; a cardigan; slippers; a hearing aid; a walking stick**. It is not always important to have as many objects as there are group members. You can have duplicates because sometimes it is interesting to have more than one participant describe the same object.

Development

The object riddles can be developed into non-rhyming poems by introducing the idea of line breaks (see Exercise 6). The resulting poem can then be given a title. (Don't use the name of the object as the title, giving away the riddle. Use a word or phrase from the body of the poem.)

10 minutes to develop a ten-syllable-per-line poem from a riddle.

Examples

Object chosen by participant: **An armchair.**

I give a little for your comfort
My front is your behind
When I'm working you're resting
I'm not hard and rigid
But soft and giving
So relax and forget that I'm supporting you.

Developed into a *free verse* poem:

GIVING
I give a little for your comfort. My
Front is your behind. When I am working
You are resting. I am not hard and
Rigid. But soft and giving. So relax
And forget that I am supporting you.

Object chosen by participant: **A bus pass** (for a workshop exploring conventional view of old age).

I am your passport to the world
But my use is restricted

So you are restricted
Till I can emerge from my plastic
And set you free in the world.

Developed into a *free verse* poem:

RESTRICTED?
I am your passport to the world, but my
Use is restricted, so you are restricted
Till I can emerge from my plastic to
Set you free into the world.

Exercise 2

Character riddle

Purpose

These riddles can be very effective when developing a workshop theme. They allow participants to role-play and try out another person's point of view. They spark discussion and help break down some conventional boundaries and preconceptions.

Method

Use character riddles after a group has done object riddles, so that they are already familiar with the technique. This is a good example of how to progress from one exercise to another. (Many of the exercises in this workbook can be related and used together to build towards a more complete exploration of a theme or issue.)

Proceed as in Exercise 1, except participants here choose characters (relating to a theme) rather than objects. For example, on the theme of 'Team Meetings', the characters I devised were: **someone at their first team meeting; someone with an important issue to raise at a team meeting; someone who always comes late to team meetings; someone who's bored at a team meeting; someone who never has anything to say at a team meeting; someone who talks too much at a team meeting; someone who disagrees with everyone else; someone who has difficulty getting his/her point across**.

Participants become the character they've picked out of the envelope and describe themselves, in four to seven sentences, in the first person, while hiding their identity. The riddles are read around and the group tries to guess the type of person described in each.

10 minutes for writing.

Example

Character chosen by participant: **A person who is always late for meetings.**

I always look embarrassed
When I come in everyone looks at me
I never sit where I want
My coffee is cold
I always miss something.

Exercise 3

ABCs

Purpose

This exercise can give a shape to memory or experience by focusing on a single concrete image. Participants feel they can risk exploring emotions because the boundaries are so clearly defined. Sharing experiences and learning about each other in this way enhance group processes, while encouraging participants to express their individuality.

Method

Give out any three consecutive letters of the alphabet. For each letter ask participants to come up with a few images, objects, food, people's names, or place names that begin with that given letter and are related to a particular topic. Topics I have used include: **my childhood; my first job; my current job**. After reading around their associations for each of the three given letters, so that the whole group can share in one another's process, ask participants to develop one association in a paragraph of prose. This paragraph is then read out.

5 minutes to list images associated with the given letters. 10 minutes to develop a prose paragraph associated with a single image.

Development

The prose produced can be successfully developed into *haiku* (see Exercise 7) or *cinquains* (see Exercise 8). Both these poetry forms further focus a piece of writing. Haiku seem more profound, cinquains more light-hearted. Having already produced a shaped piece of prose, participants can now produce a poem with the same material. The writing process is demystified and participants gain confidence in their ability to access and develop raw material for stories and poems. There is also the opportunity for participants to share emotional writing with each other that is safe because it is structured.

10 minutes to write either a haiku or cinquain.

Examples

Topic: **My childhood**

Letters: **A B C**

A: asthma, Mrs Ashburton, Alex
B: Barry, Blyth Grammar School, beer, Beatles
C: Cortina, custard, coal fire

A is for asthma. I suffered from asthma as a child. It was a real thing squeezing the breath out of me. It came and went like a hunting animal and I was frightened of it. The asthma took form at night. It came as a big cat into my room, slowly circling then pouncing at me. Its claws slashing at my body. Other nights it became a long snake. Not a fast spitting snake with fangs and poison but a sly, slithering, strong one that used its strength and length to crush the breath out of me. Doctors said these were hallucinations caused by lack of oxygen, but I knew better.

Topic: **My work**

A: application forms, ashtrays, anxiety, assignments
B: break, beds, breakfast
C: coffee, chart, computer

C is for coffee. The only thing that unites us. We all gather round the coffee machine at some time during the day. It provides chat and relief and warmth. When other things are falling apart I know the coffee will be hot and someone will be there. If not, I can always persuade someone else to share a coffee and that provides a captive audience for my troubles. I've often been someone else's captive audience too.

Exercise 4

Rant and rave

Purpose

This is an evaluative exercise which allows participants to let off steam in an offbeat way, while experiencing the different sides of an argument.

Method

Give out cards that say either 'rant' or 'rave'. Half the group responds positively to a given topic (no matter how they really feel), the other half negatively. Ask participants to write as they would speak. Repeat the exercise allowing participants to switch roles. Read around. Notice how much of the individual participant's own voice comes through. The results are often great for starting discussions.

10 minutes for each rant or rave.

Development

These 'rants and raves' can be successfully developed into haiku (see Exercise 7) or cinquains (see Exercise 8), turning the prose into brief, pithy poems. The results often sound delightfully profound.

10 minutes to write either a haiku or cinquain.

Examples

A rant on user involvement

They're never grateful that's what gets me. I try, I do everything I can and more but is there any gratitude? Of course not. It's all meetings and feedback which is always critical like, 'You shouldn't patronise us', as if I intend to. It's hard explaining complicated issues in understandable language so it can sound patronising. Does anyone see that? No, it's always criticism. If I'm doing six other things all I get is, 'You should make time for me'. I call that selfish as I'm doing things for other people but that's never recognised. I never feel valued. You all think it's great being able to slag me off but you're really giving ammunition to those who want to make things worse. What about being constructive? It never happens.

The paragraph of prose is then developed into haiku. First the participant underlines a favourite or interesting line, then translates it into a haiku.

EXPLAINING
It's hard explaining
issues, so I sometimes
sound patronising.

Exercise 5

Speaking directly

Purpose

To give participants a focused voice and help them 'energise' their writing by writing as they speak. This exercise allows participants to communicate their thoughts in a new way.

Method

Write an eight-line, non-rhyming poem addressing each line to someone (the same person) on a given topic. (It is sometimes better for the facilitator to avoid the word 'poem', and simply ask participants to write an eight-line piece.)

The whole group writes on the same topic. In a workshop I ran, I selected as a topic 'The value of older people in society', and asked participants to address each line of their piece to a teenager they knew. (The facilitator has to provide the topic, as well as the type of person addressed, who should be related to the topic. Participants think of a particular person to fit the bill.) Each line of the poem must start with that person's name and say something to that person about the topic. Each line should be a sentence in length, rather than run on to a paragraph. Read out the results.

10 minutes for writing.

Development

These poems can be developed by attempting another version in which the name at the beginning of each line is deleted. Then line breaks can be determined using ten syllables (approximately) per line (see Exercise 6). A title should be found.

It is surprising how the simple use of a name (addressing your thoughts to someone in particular) focuses writing. Often when the name is taken away, the results remain strong and direct, but become more universal. It is important to remember, however, that participants need the name in the first place. The results of this exercise will probably be something you would never have got if you had asked participants to comment, for instance, on 'The value of older people in society'.

10 minutes

Examples

Topic: **Advice I'd like to give.**

Person addressed: **My boss.**

Lisa, we like you
Lisa, you're our boss
Lisa, we need to grumble
Lisa, it's not all personal
Lisa, you should concentrate on your job
Lisa, don't try to do ours
Lisa, we need some space
Lisa, we like you

The piece is then developed into a *free verse* poem (approximately ten syllables a line, although in this case, the writer thought the first and last lines should be shorter), with the addressee's name removed and a title selected.

MY BOSS
I like you
even though you're my boss. I need to grumble.
It's nothing personal. Just do your job.
Not mine. I need some space. But Lisa,
I like you.

Exercise 6

Free verse

Purpose

To develop into a finished poem material from a previous exercise, such as prose fragments, especially lists, groups of sentences, or something that is nearly a poem. This exercise gives participants a sense of accomplishment and confidence in a growing ability to produce finished writing.

Method

Finishing or refining a piece of writing is often a nice thing to do at the end of a workshop. Ask participants to choose an exercise they have done that they would like to develop into free verse. Because it does not rhyme, free verse uses a system called 'iambic pentameter' to determine where to end one line and start another. For our purposes here, this simply means counting ten syllables a line. Ask participants to set out their poems in approximately ten syllables per line. (Ten syllables is said to resemble the rhythm of spoken English.) It may be necessary to demonstrate how to count syllables. If the measure of ten syllables ends the line in an awkward place, it is OK to try between nine and thirteen syllables.

Counting syllables in this way makes a poem flow and avoids the problem of producing something that resembles a list because each line is a sentence. When you count syllables, sentences can go over line breaks.

After a new draft is produced, ask participants to give their poem a title: choosing a word or phrase from the body of the poem is often a good idea. The results are read out.

15 minutes to develop a prose fragment into a ten-syllable-per-line poem, and to find a title.

Example

For an example of *free verse* see Exercise 1 (page 21) or Exercise 5 (page 29).

Exercise 7

Haiku

Purpose

To develop work from a previous exercise, turning prose fragments into poetry, or finding a poem within a paragraph of prose. The haiku form, in particular, has the ability to isolate an idea or thought and make it resonate with meaning. The results are often very powerful, enigmatic and profound. There is a real sense of discovery in finding a gem of a poem in a block of prose. This gives the participant a sense of accomplishment and confidence in a growing ability to produce finished writing.

Method

Finishing or refining a piece of writing is often a nice thing to do at the end of a workshop. Ask participants to choose an exercise they have done that they would like to develop into haiku. Haiku is a very short Japanese syllabic poem consisting of three lines:

- the first line has five syllables
- the second line has seven syllables
- the third line has five syllables.

It may be necessary to demonstrate how to count syllables. Because haiku is so short, participants could be asked to first underline their favourite sentence in a piece of prose and then translate that into haiku. The results are read out.

10 minutes.

Example

For an example of haiku see Exercise 4 (page 27).

Exercise 8

Cinquain

Purpose

To develop work from a previous exercise, turning prose fragments into poetry, or finding a poem within a paragraph of prose.

Method

Finishing or refining a piece of writing is often a nice thing to do at the end of a workshop. Ask participants to choose an exercise they have done that they would like to develop into a cinquain. A cinquain is a five-line, syllabic poem:

- the first line has two syllables
- the second line has four syllables
- the third line has six syllables
- the fourth line has eight syllables
- the fifth line has two syllables again.

It may be necessary to demonstrate how to count syllables.

Because of its 'rounded' form, the cinquain can often sound light-hearted. A long sentence (or two consecutive sentences) of prose often translates best into a cinquain. Ask participants to first underline their favourite sentence in a piece of prose and then translate that into a cinquain. The results are read out. (If the group has also done haiku, notice how the results feel very different.)

10 minutes.

Example

For an example of a cinquain see Exercise 28 (page 79).

Exercise 9

Lists

Purpose

A list provides participants with an easy and accessible format to respond to a variety of topics. Because of its immediacy, this is a good beginning exercise or ice-breaker.

Method

Ask participants to construct a variety of lists, consisting of four items on each list, describing themselves. For example: **four things I love; four things I hate; four things I've seen; four things I've never seen.** (It is often interesting to construct two lists simultaneously that are opposites.)

The only requirement here is that the items remain in concise list form (i.e. are not connected) and that the responses are concrete rather than abstract. Abstract nouns should be avoided. For instance, under 'four things I love', rather than listing 'happiness, peace, equality, a challenge', try to find concrete, specific images for these abstract states. Happiness might be 'walking my dog on a cold dry evening', for example. Lists can also mix in small idiosyncratic likes (e.g. 'I love the fizz in fizzy drinks'), with deeper responses. The best lists are varied. Items listed should be sentence-length, rather than a single word, because it is often easier to communicate a specific image with a phrase, or something longer. Read out the results. If the participants already know one another, the facilitator can read out the lists and group members can guess who wrote each list.

5 minutes per list (8 minutes per paired lists).

Variations

For another good ice-breaker, ask participants to list 'four things you do outside your working or professional lives'.

When I asked a group that had been meeting together professionally for some time to do this exercise, they discovered surprising similarities in hobbies and interests they had never known about at all. This was a major factor in developing group cohesion.

Another variation is to construct a list that evaluates an issue that is important to the group. By altering the list title you can retrieve feelings and evaluative responses on a variety of issues. Some of the list titles I have used that have successfully tackled issues that have been of concern to particular groups include: 'four pieces of advice you'd give someone joining this organisation'; 'four things I'm sick and tired of at work'; 'four ways in which my job has influenced the rest of my life'; 'four things I often feel at a team meeting'.

My only reservation here would be to limit the number of lists you ask participants to write in a single workshop, and also to limit the number of items on each list. My experience has been that this exercise can be tiring, or perhaps numbing, and although the first couple of lists are often inspired, list-fatigue soon sets in.

Development

You can expand this exercise by asking participants to develop one of the items on their list as the title of a short piece of prose.

List-making is connected to poetry. Before or after doing this exercise, you can hand out a poem based on a list (and there are many). I'd suggest 'Warning' by Jenny Joseph,* or 'He Loved Three Things' by Anna Akhmatova.**

It is interesting and enabling for people to see how something as simple as a list can be transformed into a poem.

Examples

Topic: **Four things I love about work**

Laughing over coffee in the morning
Closing a case
An empty in-tray
A case conference ending with everyone feeling positive

Topic: **Four things I hate about work**

Dirty coffee cups on my desk
Being shouted at with hostility
Too little time
More to do at the end of the day than at the beginning

* *The Bloodaxe Book of Contemporary Women Poets*, edited by Jeni Couzyn, Bloodaxe
** Anna Akhmatova, *Selected Poems*, Bloodaxe

Topic: **Four things I've seen**

The sun setting into the Pacific
A riot
My son playing with a fish
The Book of the North

Exercise 10

Autobiography

Purpose

An ice-breaker and an alternative way for participants to introduce themselves, this exercise also gives them a brief taste of reading out loud, because they are only reading a single sentence.

Method

Ask participants to write the first sentence of their autobiography. Read out.

5 minutes, or less.

Example

I was born in a blizzard.

Exercise 11

Ambitions

Purpose

This exercise encourages participants to express and communicate a wish or desire. It introduces a method of thinking with a pen, of digging deeper by using a writing technique based on interviewing.

Method

Ask participants to list four ambitions (small or large). Read out. Then choose one ambition and probe it by asking it four questions (i.e. by interviewing it). Ask participants to read out the ambition selected and the four questions they have asked.

5 minutes for writing the first list.
5 minutes to question one item on the first list.

Development

Participants choose their favourite question and use it as the recurring line in a *triolet*. A triolet is a simple, non-rhyming poem based on recurrence (see Exercise 15). The repeated line often creates a wistful or emotional piece of writing from unlikely subject matter.

Example

Four ambitions:

1 To be independent

2 To have a job

3 To be able to help other people rather than be helped

4 To have a holiday

Questions to ambition 1 'To be independent':

- What would I do if I were independent?
- Could I go to China?
- Is independence necessary to be happy?
- Why is independence so important?

Triolet: Repeated line: 'Is independence necessary to be happy?'

Is independence necessary to be happy?
I don't know
But I'd like to find out

Is independence necessary to be happy?
I'm not happy being dependent
So I can only try it and see

Is independence necessary to be happy?
I don't know

Exercise 12

Remembering the present

Purpose

This exercise gives participants a sense of distance, a perspective, on current issues, circumstances, concerns and problems.

Method

For each word or phrase you read out loud, ask participants to write three sentences remembering the previous year (or the previous few months) as if it were from a distance of ten (or twenty) years. The first sentence must begin with the phrase **'I remember ...'**

Participants should try to record a specific memory as each prompting word or phrase is read out by the facilitator. Then the next word or phrase is given. Six to eight words or phrases are optimal.

This is a guided exercise. The facilitator gives the prompting word or phrase and the participants respond immediately. When everyone has finished writing, or time is up, the facilitator goes on to the next word or phrase. The given words, or phrases, depend on the aims of the workshop. Phrases I have recently used include: 'I remember ... : a team meeting; the time I was late; a conflict; my desk; a letter; a laughing man; an insight'.

After all the words have been given, one participant is asked to choose his/her favourite response and read that. Then each participant, in turn, reads his/her response to that particular word. After that, another participant is asked to read his/her favourite response, and again, each participant, in turn, reads his/her response to that word, and so on.

2–3 minutes per word.

Example

Key phrases: **team meeting; the time I was late; a conflict at work; my desk.**

I remember a team meeting that took forever. Everyone seemed afraid to reach any conclusion so we went on and on. In the end nothing was resolved and I cannot even remember what the problem was.

I remember the time I was late for a ward round. Of course everyone looked as I slid through the door. My heart pounded as I anticipated the sarcastic comments to come.

I remember a conflict at work. It began as a misunderstanding about who should do what and ended up with people refusing to speak to one another. Someone should have knocked our heads together.

I remember my desk being tidy one day. I'd really worked hard cleaning it before I went on holiday. I felt uneasy with the absence of chaos.

Exercise 13

Guided fantasy

Purpose

This is an experiential exercise that allows participants to evaluate, assess, make choices and communicate likes and dislikes in a new way.

Method

The facilitator speaks to the participants asking them to close their eyes and imagine a house. This fantasy is scripted and the facilitator might want to say something like: 'You are visiting in your mind a house you would like to live in, a house where you would feel happy and comfortable. Take a moment and think about it.' Now give participants a minute to think and imagine. As you ask each question, participants respond with a sentence or two of prose rather than a single word.

- Where is this house? *(Give participants a few moments to write after each question.)*
- Imagine you're there right now. As you approach, you take in the surroundings. What's around the house?
- You're walking up to the front door. You notice a detail about the outside of the house and pause for a moment to concentrate on it. What is it?
- Now you're moving right up close to the door. You take a key out to unlock it. As the door opens, you're conscious of a smell in the house. Describe it.
- You enter the house and make your way to the kitchen. Someone's in the kitchen. Who is it? And what are they doing?
- That person asks you a question. What's the question?
- Then that person gives you something surprising. What is it? *(Remind participants to write in whole sentences.)*
- As you're leaving the room, you see an object on the kitchen table that's well known to you. Describe it.

- You tour the rest of the house you wish you lived in. In the sitting room you notice the view through the window. Describe the view.

- Standing in the middle of your favourite room, you begin to imagine something special or important that could happen here. What?

- When it's time to leave, how do you feel? Explain.

2–3 minutes per question.

Variations

Depending on the aims of the workshop, you can design your own guided fantasy about a place, using the questions above as a model. You could ask participants to fantasise about the office, day centre, meeting room, or any other facility they wish they had. Or the kind of community or neighbourhood they wish they lived in.

Example

Theme: **The day centre I wish I attended.**

- Where is the day centre?

The day centre is in the middle of town so there are other places to go if I get bored.

- Imagine you're there right now, as you approach you take in the surroundings. What's around the day centre?

The centre is surrounded by other buildings. It is on a busy road so cars and buses pass by. Of course there are ramps everywhere so I have no problem approaching.

- You're going up to the front entrance. You notice a detail about the outside of the day centre and pause for a moment to concentrate on it. What is it?

The sign. There's always a sign that marks this place as somewhere special. Just a name would be best, not a social services logo or, even worse, words identifying this as a place for the disabled.

- Now you're moving right up close to the door. You open the door, as it opens you're conscious of a smell in the day centre. Describe it.

The smell isn't institutional. It smells like freshly brewed coffee.

- You enter the day centre and make your way to the kitchen. Someone's in the kitchen. Who is it? And what are they doing?

Staff. They're cheerful, making coffee, tea and toast. They know my name and make jokes. They even laugh at my jokes.

- That person asks you a question. What's the question?

'How are you today?' Then they'll listen to my reply.

- Then that person gives you something surprising. What is it?

She gives me a plant. Plants should be everywhere here. This plant vibrates with life and greenness. I have to decide where it will live.

- As you're leaving the room you see an object on the kitchen table that's well known to you. Describe it.

A huge teapot. This teapot is made of metal and is dull with overuse. It can produce enough tea for twenty people. The teapot provides comfort, talk and pleasure. It tells the time as it always appears at 11am and 3pm.

- You tour the rest of the day centre you wish you attended. In the lounge you notice the view from the window. Describe the view.

Things are happening in the real world. The view is interesting to look at. People shop, rush, look at their watch waiting for someone who's late. Cars try to hurry but have to crawl, their drivers wishing they'd walked. Sometimes people look in here but quickly turn away embarrassed as they realise what they're looking at.

- Standing in the middle of your favourite room, you begin to imagine something special or important that could happen here. What is it?

I'm talking to my key worker about leaving. I might have a job. She's advising caution, telling me that I can come back if things don't work out. I'm impatient and just want to go, although part of me wants to stay in the comfort and security of this place.

- When it's time to leave, how do you feel? Explain.

I'm pleased to be back in the world again but I know there will be problems. There are so many things I cannot do that I sometimes forget the things I can do. I remember that I'll be back in two days.

Exercise 14

Letter writing

Purpose

A problem-solving exercise that also allows participants to give vent to some negative feelings towards, complaints about, or uneasiness with the workplace and/or services. This exercise was first devised for a workshop for older users of a service who were often reticent and unwilling to evaluate the service. The format of letter-writing seems very accessible because it is familiar to people who have no experience with other forms of writing.

Method

Ask participants to write a brief letter to a friend or relation (not an agony aunt) asking advice on a problem (large or small) at work, in the community, with a service, with neighbours, etc. (The facilitator must tailor this exercise to the needs of the group and the issues that concern them.) Without letting on what is coming, be sure to ask participants to try to write legibly.

The finished letters are collected and handed out again at random, making sure that none of the participants gets back the letter they wrote.

Everyone must now answer the letter they have been randomly given as if they were the person it was addressed to, and offer the required advice.

When reading out, each participants reads both the letter they received and the answer given.

10 minutes to write the first letter.
10 minutes to write the answer.

(This exercise usually prompts a lot of discussion and I would advise facilitators to leave plenty of time around it. In addition, the letters produced are often longer than the writing that's usually done in these workshops, and every participant must read two letters out, so a lot of time must be allocated for reading out loud.)

Example

Topic: **Day care.**

The letter I received:

Dear Mary,

I am writing to ask your advice about a little problem I'm having with the day centre. As you know, mum goes there for two days each week. It's a real blessing to me as I know she's safe and the staff are all lovely. She goes at half past nine in the morning and is brought home at about half past three in the afternoon. That gives me plenty of time to clean up, get the shopping and sometimes to sit with my feet up for half an hour!

I know mum's happy and well cared for when she's at the centre. The only problem is that when she's brought home she's usually wet. She wears incontinence pads and they've soaked through and wet all her clothes. I have to change her as soon as she comes home and that sometimes puts her in a foul mood for the evening. If her pad was changed before she left the centre then the evening would be so much easier.

My problem is should I say anything. I don't want the staff to think I'm ungrateful and I do know they all work very hard and don't have much time. I don't want them to think of me as someone who makes a mountain out of a molehill. I'm also a little worried that some of them might take against mum if they think I've complained and made a fuss. So what do you think dear? I'm getting quite worked up thinking about this.

Love,

Ann

My reply:

Dear Ann,

Of course you should speak to the staff about this. Your mum shouldn't be wet and you shouldn't have to change her as soon as she gets home. The only real questions are who to speak to and how to bring this up.

Has your mum got a special member of staff who looks after her? Is there someone at the centre you feel you can talk to? Do you know the manager? You have to ask yourself these questions and then decide who is the best person to speak to. It would be better if it was someone who knows your mum so her key worker would be a good choice. However, you must decide who you'd be most comfortable speaking to.

The next question is how to bring this up. I think you could start with a general question about her incontinence. Ask something like, 'Is my mum wet a lot of the time?' The answer you get can help you bring up your concern. You could say you're concerned because she's always wet when she gets home. Ask if they know that already and if there's anything they can do about it. I think you can ask these questions without being confrontational. Whatever happens don't be put off. You know there's something that can be done. They could change your mum's pad before she leaves. If the person you speak to doesn't suggest that then you'll have to. If you're not happy with the answer you get then you should see the manager. I do think though that a little prompting from you will help and that this problem can easily be resolved. Remember, you're right here. She shouldn't be coming home wet.

Let me know what happens and good luck.

Love,

Mary

Exercise 15

Triolet

Purpose

Like haiku and cinquains, a triolet is a poetry form that does not depend on rhyming. Unlike haiku and cinquains, however, a triolet is not based on counting syllables, but on recurrent lines. The results are like a song (the recurring lines often sound very poignant) so that translating another piece of writing into this form is a satisfying exercise. The form itself is easy to complete and gives participants a sense of accomplishment. It is also a good way to extend any exercise you want to probe deeper.

Method

A triolet is an eight-line unrhyming poem. The first line reoccurs as the fourth and seventh line. Filling in the blanks, you must make up the rest of the lines. The second line reoccurs as the eighth line. (I'd suggest you photocopy and give out this model to participants.)

Ask participants to choose a short sentence from the writing they've already done. Use this sentence as the recurring line.

1...(Repeat as line 4 and 7)

2...(Repeat as line 8)

3...

4...(Same as line 1)

5...

6...

7...(Same as line 1)

8...(Same as line 2)

Read around.

10 minutes' writing time. (Leave extra time to choose sentences and explain technique.)

Variations

A question works well as the recurring line. You might use an interview technique (see Exercise 11) to provide a question, or simply suggest participants ask themselves a single question about the issues in a particular piece of writing they have already done. This allows the writer to extend a particular idea by probing into it more deeply.

Example

For an example of a triolet, see Exercise 11 (page 38).

Section 2

Challenging

Exercise 16

Alliteration

Purpose

This is a useful exercise for developing a workshop theme, or evaluating an issue. I have been told by participants that this exercise is especially good for discovering and developing ideas and views they might not have known they held, or for finding new slants on familiar issues. While concentrating on restrictive rules and instructions, participants may find themselves taking more risks with the content.

Method

Alliteration is the repetition of initial sounds (first letters) in adjacent words. Decide on the letter you want repeated. The whole group should use the same letter. (For this exercise participants might like to see a photocopied example.) Ask participants to write a long alliterative sentence of their own, using as many words as possible beginning with the given letter on the same (given) topic. The topic should be based on issues or processes you want to examine in the workshop. ('Coming out of hospital' and 'Weekly team meetings' are examples of two topics I have used successfully in workshops.) The results are then read aloud so that everyone can check they've got the hang of alliteration. Two more letters are offered, one at a time, and participants continue to produce alliterative sentences on the same topic. The topic does not change, only the letter. Then all three sentences are read out in a final read-around.

5 minutes per sentence writing time.

Example

Topic: **Team meetings.**

Repeated letters: **A, B, C.**

A

A meeting always arrives at the most awful time when I have at least ten absolutely urgent things to do and again I argue as I'm frustrated.

B

'Better be on my best behaviour,' I think, because my beastly remarks are taken seriously by both my best friends here.

C

Cannot we call a vote rather that coolly create more creaking discussion that ceased being creative a long time ago?

Exercise 17

Ordinary objects

Purpose

This exercise might be particularly successful with a diverse group of participants, perhaps users and workers, as some of the aims are related to imagining another's point of view and democratising a group.

Method

Describe an ordinary object (it is often good to actually produce the object) from the point of view of a person very different from yourself. This new identity is randomly chosen from an envelope containing strips of paper on which identities are written. (Some ideas I have used that have worked well, depending on the organisation and the goals of the workshop, include: **a child; a teenager; a bind person; a homeless person; an unemployed person; a retired person; an older person; a social worker; a GP.**) With this exercise it is not usually necessary to have as many identities in the envelope as group members: it is good to duplicate the identities in the envelope so that you get different participants with the same identity. As you read around, the group may want to try to guess the assumed identity of the writer.

10 minutes to produce the paragraph of prose.

Example

Object: **A bathtub**

Identity: **A homeless person**

A bath in my dreams is filled with sweet smelling foam. It waits my pleasure as I can decide when to take it. It is hot and steamy and cleans my cares as well as my body. The bath is long with a space for a radio to play music that helps the bath provide relaxation. The bath does not hurry me but tells me to take as long as I like.

The bath smells so sweet, like spring, and imparts that smell into my soul. My dream slams shut as the attendant shouts at me for taking too long. 'Don't you know, there's twenty others for a bath this morning?'

Exercise 18

Headlines

Purpose

Evaluating a familiar issue or situation in a new way.

Method

Make up a newspaper-type headline that refers to issues surrounding work, or workshop themes. '*"I will not be a burden," cries Newcastle pensioner*', for example. Ask participants to write a short newspaper article that goes with the headline. (For something more challenging you could give them a precise word count, 25 words for example.) Read around.

10–15 minutes' writing time.

Example

Given headline: **'Social services team sorts itself out'.**

Yesterday the infamous Area 6 Social Services team decided enough was enough. They gathered together in secret to devise a plan that would end the feuding 'once and for all.' Team leader, Pauline Crust, said: 'The whole team wants to change and I intend making sure it does.' A spokesperson for the rebels (unnamed) commented: 'Ms Crust can only carry out her plan with our assistance. We want harmony as much as anyone else but we have demands that must be met before any progress can be made.'

Analysts later forecast 'tears before laughter' at Area 6.

Exercise 19

Name acrostic

Purpose

This exercise is a good ice-breaker, and a unique way for the participants to introduce themselves, while experiencing creative writing for the first time. An acrostic must be done according to detailed directions, but the results are startling.

Method

Ask participants to write the letters of their first name down the left-hand side of a piece of paper. (If their name is very short, they can use a middle name or a last name as well.) Each line of the acrostic has to begin with the appropriate letter and say something about the participant in question. The whole acrostic can be one sentence, but each line should not start a new sentence. The name written down the left-hand side of the paper should not be repeated in the acrostic, but it can be the title.

The way to begin is to write a short paragraph about yourself, then as if you were doing a puzzle, or a brain teaser, try to fit the sentences in your paragraph into the acrostic form. The results are read out as each member introduces himself or herself.

10 minutes.

Variations

You can ask participants to construct an acrostic poem using any word or phrase that is relevant to the group, or the focus of your workshop. Everyone gets the same word. The results are read out loud.

Any exercise in this workbook can be extended by asking the participant to find a word or short phrase in a piece they have written that seems important to them. (Or ask them to choose a title for a piece they have written.) Using that word, or phrase, or title as the basis for an acrostic poem, they complete the extended exercise. The results are read out.

Example

Name acrostic

To construct a name acrostic, begin by writing a short paragraph about yourself:

'My name is Phil and I'm a social worker. I'm married with two children: a boy, 13, and a girl, 11. I usually enjoy my work but it can get a bit frustrating. I enjoy sport. I play football, squash and tennis. I like the way physical activity gets rid of my frustrations. I also enjoy gardening, going to the cinema and going to sunny places for a holiday.'

Translate your paragraph into acrostic form, trying to avoid a sentence per line:

PHILIP
Playing football, squash and tennis
Hardly leaves time for work.
I enjoy sport. I
Like the way
It gets rid of my frustration.
Perhaps making me a better social worker.

Object acrostic

Although you're not supposed to mention your name in the name acrostic, participants found it impossible not to mention the object name in the object acrostic.

Topic: **My desk.**

Descriptive paragraph:

'I like everything on my desk to be very neat and tidy. I feel that I can only think clearly when my desk is ordered. Sometimes I'm anxious about it. The only one who can leave half full cups of coffee on my desk, is me. When I get busy, my desk is a mess.'

Object acrostic:

MY DESK
Messy desks are something I hate.
You need to have a tidy
Desk in order to think clearly.
Everything neat and tidy.
Sometimes I'm so anxious about neatness, I could
Kick myself.

Exercise 20

Anagram

Purpose

To help participants articulate in prose, not only their needs, but their 'what-if' wishes around a given issue.

Method

Ask participants to write their full names (including middle names and maiden names) on a piece of paper. Using some, not all, the letters in their name, they now create a new name for themselves, changing gender if they wish. Read around immediately to hear the different names. (Most participants can think of quite a few new names with the letters available, in the time given. It is fun to hear them all, but a favourite must be chosen in order to complete the exercise.)

It is interesting how a new name suggests a new identity. Participants are now asked to describe, in a paragraph of prose, what this newly named character, this alter-ego, would do that they cannot do, or feel constrained from doing.

Then, in a second paragraph of prose, participants are asked to consider this alter ego's relationship to an issue that needs evaluating by the group. For example, in a recent workshop I ran, participants were asked how this alter ego would respond to 'Recent changes in the service they provide'.

Both paragraphs are read out together.

5 minutes for the construction of the anagram.
5 minutes to complete each paragraph.
15 minutes for the whole exercise.

Development

This exercise can be expanded into an acrostic. Ask participants to write an acrostic (see Exercise 19) using the alter ego's name and mentioning something about his/her character.

Example

Real name: Paul Scott
Anagram: Pat Lout

- What this character would do that I cannot

I say what I think unlike that wimp Paul Scott. People either love me or hate me and frankly I don't care which. Everyone is on edge at meetings in case I say something awful. Sometimes I do, sometimes I don't. It all depends on what needs to be said. I hate the way everyone else says what they feel they ought to say and not what they really think. Problems would never be discussed or indeed solved if it weren't for me. Everyone would be too frightened of upsetting someone. Why do they all take everything so personally?

- How this character would respond to: 'Recent changes in the service'

What changes? It seems to me that no one is doing anything different. Of course, the forms we fill in are different and we constantly make mistakes because of that. My point is that everyone's attitude is the same. If we asked those on the receiving end of our services what they thought, I'm sure they wouldn't have noticed any change to the service they get. So I'll ask again, what changes?

Anagram acrostic

Perhaps I'm too out spoken.
All I do is
Talk plainly.

Look at the rest
Of you.
Using polite words
To avoid trouble.

Exercise 21

Writing from the senses

Purpose

This exercise encourages thinking and communicating using similes. (A simile is a figure of speech in which two dissimilar things are compared by the use of like or as). Having to translate familiar thoughts, impressions, judgements and evaluations into this new mode of expression yields surprising, hopefully insightful, results.

Method

Participants are asked to recall a specific event related to the theme or aims of the workshop. (For example, I once asked a group to recall 'The first whole systems meeting they ever attended'. Later I asked them to recall 'The best whole systems meeting they ever attended', then, 'The worst'.)

Participants are then asked to record in a single complete sentence, for each of the five senses:

1. What the meeting (or event) *looked like* ...

(Something that stands out that they saw, or a colour associated in their mind with the meeting.) If participants cannot specifically recall anything of this nature, encourage them to make something up that communicates, or captures, the atmosphere. This is a very important point because this exercise is primarily about making similes. When using a simile, we are comparing one thing with something else. What we lose in exactness, we gain in emotional subjective content. In this exercise we are after emotional, not literal, truth. For example, 'At my first whole systems meeting, the light was as bright as sunshine on snow'. It might be necessary to give this, or another example of a simile.

I would recommend that participants read out after the first sentence is completed, so that everyone can check they have got the hang of writing similes. After this, they can complete the next four sentences without stopping to hear the results until the end. Give out the directions, sentence by sentence, and wait while participants write down their responses.

2. What the meeting *sounded like* ...

(What could be heard at the meeting or event, any sounds other than voices that you can recall, that you can associate with that meeting, or compare that meeting with. For example, 'It sounded like a gaggle of geese.')

3. What the meeting *felt like* ...

(Physically, employing the sense of touch rather than what it felt like emotionally.)

4. What the meeting *smelled like* ...

5. What the meeting *tasted like* ...

(This one really has to be imagined.) 'It tasted dry as days-old bread.'

6. And finally, the most memorable thing someone said to you on that occasion (or might have said) in direct speech ...

Read out the results.

About 2 minutes per sentence. Watch as people write and introduce the next sentence when they seem to have finished.

Example

Topic: **The first whole systems meeting I ever attended.**

1. The meeting glowed like radioactive waste
2. It sounded like the sea on a stormy day
3. The meeting felt like a wet sponge
4. It smelled like grass after rain
5. The meeting tasted like yesterday's reheated take-away curry
6. 'Sorry, this must mean nothing to you. Can I explain what's going on?' (I wish)

Exercise 22

Job description

Purpose

Because of the indirect way in which it is constructed, this exercise allows participants to make judgements and to complain with a vigour they might ordinarily shy away from.

Method

Ask participants to make a mental list of people in their lives they like, and people they don't like. Choosing one person they like and one person they dislike, ask participants to describe (in a paragraph of prose for each) a job in your organisation, field, community, for the person they like, then a job for the person they dislike.

10 minutes.

Example

My friend would have the job of organising outings for the clients. She is a good organiser so would be able to do the job well. She would really be appreciated by everyone as outings are so popular; they break the boredom for both clients and staff. Everyone likes getting out, and the staff who don't go can get on with their work undisturbed. This job would, of course, come with a budget that would allow imaginative outings. My friend would go on them all but her responsibility would have ended with the organisation so she could simply enjoy the trips.

The person I don't like would have the job of day-to-day management of the centre. She would have to ensure we had enough staff and that they had what they need to run the centre. She would deal with complaints and difficult clients. Her day would be spent trying to make ends meet without enough resources.

Exercise 23

Diaries

Purpose

This exercise allows participants to put themselves in a different position, or try out a new identity, and hopefully make discoveries of an insightful nature through sustained writing. It is a flexible exercise and can be used to reflect many workshop aims and themes.

Method

Ask participants to write a diary entry, for a specific day, for someone else. Depending on the nature of the group, a variety of identities can be selected from an envelope containing labels with various identities, such as: **an older person, a carer, a single parent, a social worker, a disabled person, a GP**. Workers can be asked to write entries for users, and vice versa. In a workshop I led in Newcastle on 'Images of older people and their contribution to society', I asked a group of professionals to write a diary entry for themselves for 11 September 2028 (when they would be older people themselves).

After choosing an identity, ask participants to begin this exercise by writing a list of some things they imagine this person might do on a particular day. Then ask them to pick the most interesting, or intriguing, thing on the list, and to begin their diary entry (a few paragraphs of prose) with that, rather than beginning with waking up in the morning.

As in the riddles, group members can listen to the diary entries and try to guess what identity the various participants have chosen.

10–15 minutes.

Example

Write a diary entry for yourself for 11 September 2028

List

- woke late
- got dressed (slowly)

- breakfast
- listened to radio
- read newspaper
- lunch
- went to Russian class
- shopping
- cooked dinner
- took dog out

Diary entry

11 September 2028

I went to my Russian class today. Having lots of time to work at it seems to compensate for my failing memory. I now buy a Russian newspaper every day. I'm more interested in day-to-day life than in world events, so I turn to the 'lifestyle' sections first. I can understand most of what is written but conversation is still difficult if it is fast.

The class is interesting. I am the oldest student and at the end I smirk a little as everyone else hurries off to their busy lives. I dawdle, look around, stop off for some shopping. I can only carry a little since I stopped driving, so I take every opportunity to buy food.

I have become quite good at cooking Indian food. I love the fact that some meals take days to prepare. I didn't have the time when I worked, but now time is no problem.

Exercise 24

A simple action

Purpose

This exercise allows participants to put themselves in a different position, or try out a new identity, and hopefully make discoveries of an insightful nature through sustained writing.

Method

Ask participants to write about a simple action taken in a specific place from an identity different from their own. For example, 'I climbed the stairs to my flat'; or 'I fell asleep at the pictures'. Everyone should have the same given action. Identities are chosen at random from a prepared envelope, depending on the group and the workshop goals. For example: **a carer; a disabled person; an alcoholic; a homeless person; a manager; a person who cannot speak English; a very tall person; a very short person.**

Write a paragraph of prose describing this simple action from the identity selected. Read out and discuss. The group might want to try to guess what identity the various participants have chosen.

10 minutes' writing time.

Example

Action: **Falling asleep at the cinema.**

Person: **A carer.**

Wednesdays are the days I have some time. Mum goes to the day centre so I can indulge myself. I usually only have a coffee after the shopping as I have the house to clean when I've got some time on my own but today I really indulge myself and go to see a film. In the afternoon, I can't believe how I'm spoiling myself. I sit down in the cinema and immediately feel comfortable. There are no endless questions: 'What's happening?', 'What's going on?', 'Where am I?', 'Who are you?' There are no smells of stale urine that never go away. The cinema is empty. Everyone else is busy and I feel as if I'm the only person in the world with time to myself. As the lights dim and the credits roll I drift off to sleep. I know I'm missing the film but I think that undisturbed sleep is my real desire.

Exercise 25

Heroes

Purpose

An exercise with an unfamiliar starting point that hopefully yields an evaluating response.

Method

Ask participants to write down the name of their childhood hero, real or fictitious. Read around. Now, in a paragraph of prose, everyone is asked to imagine that hero doing their particular job, or imagine that person at a team meeting, or in any situation that focuses on the aims or themes of your workshop.

At a workshop I led in Newcastle for retired or elderly users who attended whole systems meetings – the focus was on whether or not they felt included in the process – I asked people to 'imagine their childhood hero walking into a whole systems meeting'.

The results are read out.

10 minutes.

Example

Childhood hero: **Davey Crockett**

Topic: **Imagine your childhood hero walking into a whole systems meeting.**

As Davey Crockett sauntered into the whole systems meeting the room fell silent. He took off his beaver skin hat and laid his trusty rifle on the table. 'Howdy folks,' he said. 'Let's do the business.' People eyed the rifle as the meeting got under way.

Soon Davey stood up. 'I can see I'm in the wrong place,' he drawled. 'I'm an all-action impulsive kind of guy. All this talk clutters up my head. You don't need me here.' As he turned to leave everyone protested telling him that whole systems is inclusive and that we can talk about how to use his unique talents. Davey silenced these protests as he lifted his rifle. 'No,' he said finally, 'I'm not right here. Do you need someone to kill a bear?' He looked round and smiled as he saw he had made his point.

Exercise 26

Role models

Purpose

An exercise that uses the past, and past experiences, to evaluate issues in the present.

Method

Ask participants to recall someone who gave them a pleasant or unpleasant impression of authority (responsibility, leadership, co-operation). In a recent workshop I led in Newcastle on 'Images of old age and the contribution of older people to society', I asked a group to recall 'a person who gave them a positive image of old age'.

Begin by noting, in a sentence of prose:

- Something this person always said, or a sound associated with this person.
- Something this person always did – a habit, mannerism, gesture or action associated with this person.
- One object associated with this person.
- One object never to be associated with this person.

From these writing notes, produce a paragraph of prose about this positive or negative role model. Read out.

5 minutes to complete writing notes.
10 minutes to write.

Development

Construct an acrostic (see Exercise 19) using your role model's full name, saying something about how you met them to explore further their influence on you.

Example

Recall a person who gave you a positive image of old age and note in a sentence of prose:

- Something this person always said, or a sound associated with this person:

  Tapping of a white stick – he had gone blind aged seventy-one.

- Something this person always did – a habit, a mannerism, gesture or action associated with this person:

  He closed his eyes when he was thinking.

- One object associated with this person:

  He constantly listened to the radio or tapes on a Walkman. He needed headphones as his hearing was so acute that he was distracted by background noise without them.

- One object never to be associated with this person:

  A guide dog.

From these notes, produce a paragraph of prose about this positive role model.

Sam Peel was seventy-nine and looked it. His health was generally poor and he had been blind for eight years. He didn't get out much, but spent his days alone. I was asked to visit after neighbours expressed concern at his ability to cope. He roared with laughter as I explained the reason for my visit. The concerns about his ability to cope; the fact that he must be lonely and understimulated. Sam told me that he'd never been happier. His daughter visited him once a week and brought his shopping. He didn't like depending on her, but knew he had to. He spent his time listening to the radio or to classic novels on audiotape.

'I know things I've never known before,' he said. He demonstrated this by quizzing me on current affairs, and it was obvious he knew far more than I did. He told me that he not only listened to news, plays and novels but he also had time to think about them. His problems, he told me, were not the most important things in his life.

Construct an acrostic from that person's name:

So, you think you can
Arrange my life. He said to
Me. I might look like I need you,

Perhaps I do. But
Each to his own. I have
Enough of everything I need to
Last the rest of my life.

Section 3

Most challenging

Exercise 27

Inventions

Purpose

A problem-solving exercise, that takes a 'what if?' approach.

Method

Ask participants to dream up an invention (realistic or fantastic) that will solve an existing work-related problem. The invention must be an object or device, but the problem it solves may be more abstract, even hard to pin down. 'Our inability to work together' could be the given problem, for instance. The invention that would solve this problem should be described in a paragraph of prose, then given a name. Read around.

10–15 minutes' writing time.

Development

Using the name of their invention, ask participants to construct an acrostic poem that says something about the device (see Exercise 19).

10–15 minutes to write the acrostic.

Example

My invention makes space and quiet. When the centre is full, it will make new rooms that are not full of the sounds of screaming kids. It makes a place where users and staff can talk about ordinary things like East Enders. It is called a 'spacer'.

The name 'Spacer' developed into an acrostic poem.

SPACER

Save us from the noise
Please. Let us be normal
At least for five minutes
Can we try to forget
Every horrible thing about our
Rotten lives?

Exercise 28

Place

Purpose

An evaluative exercise that can tease out feelings and ideas about work and the working environment that are otherwise difficult to reach, or perhaps user reactions to services and the place in which they are provided.

Method

Ask participants to write a paragraph of prose describing a place (one place for the whole group, chosen by the facilitator) and communicating a mood, picked out at random from a prepared envelope. Places I have used in this exercise, depending on the group, include: **an office; a community centre; a meeting room**. Moods I have written on strips of paper for the envelope might include: **anger; chaos; harmony; fear; loneliness; comradeship; safety; vulnerability**. The idea is to describe the place and communicate a mood in your description. Moods should be communicated regardless of how the participant actually feels about the particular place. In this way we begin to tease out what makes people feel happy, safe, secure, or insecure in certain environments. When reading their responses around, the group should try to guess the mood suggested. After everyone has read, you can compare the various descriptions (remember they're all describing the same place) in a discussion.

10–15 minutes' writing time.

Development

These paragraphs can be successfully developed into haiku (see Exercise 7) or cinquains (see Exercise 8). The brief and pithy poems that result often sound profound and can be discussed and pondered.

10 minutes to write either a haiku or cinquain.

Example

Place: **The office.**

Mood chosen by participant: **Fear.**

The office is quiet. I am first in, as usual. Why can't anyone else be on time? Usually I relish this quiet but today it is strangely unsettling. I don't make myself a drink but wander about looking for something. I don't know what, but I feel it's here somewhere. A noise startles me. I look around but can't find what caused it. 'Just the boiler' I tell myself. I look at my watch wishing someone else will arrive but no-one's due in for another half hour. <u>The flip-chart is still in the middle of the room, its accusing lists of things to do stand out in red.</u> I bump into Jim's desk looking so untidy that for a moment I want to sort it out for him. I make myself put the kettle on. The sounds help me relax. It's just a normal day after all, isn't it?

A cinquain developed from a paragraph of prose on place. First the participant underlines a favourite or interesting line, then translates it into a cinquain. A title has been selected from the body of the poem.

THINGS TO DO
Flip-chart
In the middle
Of the room. Accusing
List of things to do in bright red
Stands out.

Exercise 29

Acrostic sentence

Purpose

A more difficult acrostic, this exercise encourages fresh responses to familiar issues by asking the participant to focus on a demanding technique. Participants ought to have already done an ordinary acrostic before trying this. It certainly should not be used at the beginning of a workshop, as it is probably the most difficult exercise in this workbook.

Method

Select a ten-to-twelve word sentence from a newspaper or a book. Choose a sentence without names of individuals, but with plenty of interesting words and concrete nouns. Here is one from a newspaper item I have used successfully: *'Dinosaurs may have cracked their tails like huge bullwhips to woo lovers.'* Ask participants to copy out this sentence and then to write each consecutive word down the left-hand side of a piece of paper, as with the letters in an ordinary acrostic. A topic that has nothing to do with the content of the sentence is then given out. For example, 'Are we are finally addressing the needs of the community?' was the topic I gave out to go with the sentence about dinosaurs. Using each subsequent word of the newspaper sentence as the first word of each line, participants wrote an acrostic on this topic.

Each line of the acrostic ought not to be longer than a single line on the page, before participants have to introduce the next new word. As in other acrostics, each first word need not begin a new sentence. The results are read out.

15 minutes.

Example

Newspaper sentence: **'Dinosaurs may have cracked their tails like huge bullwhips to woo lovers'**

Topic: **Are we finally addressing the needs of the community?**

Dinosaurs are extinct as we
may be if we don't
have the courage of our convictions.
cracked walls and peeling paint in
their day centre seem to mean that
tails are wagging dogs. We don't
like working here. It must be a
huge disappointment to have to come.
bullwhips will be needed soon
to drive clients in. We should
woo them with flowers like
lovers so they would feel really wanted.

Exercise 30

Two minutes

Purpose

A more demanding ice-breaker and introduction, perhaps for a more sophisticated group or a group who has already had some experience with these workshops. Asking people to highlight what is important in their lives, without really thinking (in two minutes) can produce some interesting responses.

Method

Ask participants to write their autobiography in two minutes. Read out.

2 minutes exactly by the clock.

Variations

Ask participants to respond instantly, in two minutes, to an issue or a single selected word. (The issue or buzz word will, of course, depend on specific aims of the group.) This is almost like free association, or automatic writing. Tell participants that spelling and grammar are not important, but that they must keep their pen moving for two minutes. If they go blank, a technique developed from automatic writing is to repeat the last word they have written before drying up, over and over again, until they can move on. The results can be very strange and unpredictable. Participants should not be required to read these pieces out. Instead, they might be asked to find the most surprising, intriguing, unusual sentence or fragment in what they have written, read that and explain why it surprised them.

Example

Autobiography

I was born in Blyth. My schooldays were fun. I became a hippie at thirteen and suffered because of it in a town where it was daring to like Bob Dylan. As soon as I could, I left the suffocating home town and moved South. I spent time travelling Europe, then settled down aged twenty-seven. I married and we had two children who have been wearing me out ever since. They're good kids and I'm very proud of them and I love them to bits but, boy, do they tire me out. So after they were born lots of things stopped. I was going to do all kinds of wonderful things but didn't. Now they're older I can see that my time is coming again. I hope I'm still up to it.

Exercise 31

Vocabulary

Purpose

This exercise requires participants to closely follow a set of rules based on a randomly selected vocabulary, while writing about a topic that calls for judgement or evaluation. In this way, evaluation is removed from familiar jargon. Everyone is asked to think and communicate in an unfamiliar way. This is a good democratising exercise particularly when participants are selected from different disciplines or when users and workers get together in a workshop.

Method

Short newspaper items must be preselected in order to do this exercise. I'd recommend cutting brief items from the newspaper – weather, travel, fashion, or any short article that offers a rich vocabulary about a particular topic is good.

Hand these out (each participant gets a different article) and ask participants to read the article they have been given and underline their ten favourite words, or the ten most intriguing or interesting words they can find. Using all these ten words, participants now write about, or evaluate, a given issue in a paragraph or two of prose. For example, I recently asked a group to write on 'What the whole systems approach means to you', using vocabulary gleaned from a variety of newspaper clippings. The results are read out.

15 minutes.

Example

Select ten favourite or most interesting words from the newspaper cutting overleaf and underline them.

Deeper, darker

Jazz CD

Martin Gayford

Mose Allison
Gimcracks and Gewgaws
(Blue Note 7243 8 23211)

"IN the whole wide world there is only one/And I'm the only one," sang Mose Allison on *The Seventh Son*. And it's true. He is a unique performer. No one else duplicates that combination of bebop, jazz piano and laidback, drawling, Deep South voice. Nor does anyone else write lyrics with the same blend of street-corner patter and sardonic reflections on life and death.

The voice is now deeper, and darker than when he first recorded in the Fifties, while his instrumental style has become more intricate and percussive, with swirling, Cajun rhythms. At 70, his song writing attention seems to be turning towards last things.

"What will it be, the thing that actually kills you?" one jaunty little number starts. There are dark, even bitter undertones ("Well, an old man/Ain't nothing in the USA").

But these are belied by the vitality of the music. This is Allison's best album in years. He is assisted by a marvellous band including master drummer Paul Motian and Russell Malone on guitar. Mark Shim pops up from time to time with suitably rich and bluesy tenor solos. Mose himself is on great form.

Topic: **'Getting older'**

Words selected: **unique, bebop, jazz, laid-back, lyrics, street-corner, bitter, Cajun, jaunty, bluesy.**

Getting older isn't what it was. Here am I, ready to be more **laid-back** in my life when all these opportunities arise for older people. Learn **jazz,** Japanese or landscape painting in all that spare time. I have to say I'm **bitter** about it all. No relaxing days in front of the television; my schedule seems as busy as it was when I worked.
I thought I was **unique** but I keep bumping into stressed elders rushing from class to class trying to master new skills before it's too late. There's a buzz about being old. **Bebop** rather than fox-trot. My children think I'll end up out on the **street-corner** because I spend so much on leisure activity. I'm still in there, though. Singing a **jaunty** song (from the **Cajun** class on Tuesday mornings). Eventually I'll have to stop because of physical frailty or death. My singing will cease or turn **bluesy**. That's an idea. A blues appreciation group.

Exercise 32

End-word rhymes

Purpose

An unusual exercise that encourages creative thinking and often yields fresh responses, particularly when used to evaluate familiar issues.

Method

This exercise takes a little preparation. Preselect a short rhyming (or non-rhyming) poem or the first verse of a poem. You are looking for something from four to eight lines in length. I would recommend Robert Browning or W.H. Auden. Photocopy the poem, then ink out everything but the end word of each line. (Ink out the title and author too.) Now photocopy this version. Hand out these photocopies (everyone gets the same poem) and ask participants to fill in the blanks on a given subject, related to the aim of the workshop. Read out.

15 minutes.

Example

Poem: Song from 'Pippa Passes' by Robert Browing

The year's at the spring	spring
And day's at the morn;	morn
Morning's at seven;	seven
The hill-side's dew-pearled;	dew-pearled
The lark's on the wing;	wing
The snail's on the thorn:	thorn
God's in his heaven –	heaven
All's right with the world!	world

Subject: **What prevents me being positive at work?**

When winter turns to **spring**
I wake early each **morn**
Always before **seven**
And look out on a **dew-pearled**
Lawn. I stir myself and take to **wing;**
To arrive before the day's first **thorn**
Pricks my pleasure. Too many calls. **Heaven**
Would be a phone-free **world.**

Exercise 33

Photographs

Purpose

This exercise tries to make abstract concepts concrete. One general aim of this workbook is to shun abstract nouns (such as 'co-operation', 'equality', 'hostility') and replace them with concrete images that illustrate and redefine those abstract words we use almost automatically. This exercise is, in a way, like going back to basics and asking ourselves what we really mean.

Method

Ask group members to imagine a magazine or newspaper photograph with the caption, 'co-operation'. (Or any abstract concept you want to highlight, redefine, or evaluate in your workshop. Other abstract nouns I have used for this exercise include: **stress; leadership; decision-making.**) The caption doesn't have to be an abstract noun at all, but whatever word or phrase applies to the aims and themes of your workshop. A magazine or newspaper photo is not always the best option either. You might prefer to ask the group to imagine that the photo is a snapshot taken at work. I leave this up to you.

Ask group members to describe this photo as if they were looking at it right now. These descriptions should be written in present tense. (Present tense helps new writers focus on the here and now, making their writing more concrete.) If the photo is a snapshot, participants can choose to include themselves in the photo, or not.

In order to help group members visualise this photograph, ask them to respond to the questions below in a complete sentence, or two, of prose. Remind them to write in present tense. After each question is asked, give them time to write.

- Where's the photo been taken?
- Who's in the photo?
- What expressions are on their faces?
- What are they doing?
- How are they dressed?
- What are they holding in their hands?
- What's in the background?
- Is it day or night?
- What single detail is most interesting?
- There is one thing in this photo that doesn't belong. What is it?

If participants have written in complete sentences in answer to these questions, the results ought to read fluently as a single piece of writing. Try it out. Read around.

About two minutes per sentence. Watch as people write, and introduce the next sentence when they seem to have finished.

Example

Snapshot entitled **'Co-operation'**

- Where's the photo been taken?

  The photo is of our office.

- Who's in the photo?

  I am in the photo with my colleague Paul and our manager Sue.

- What expressions are on their faces?

  We have serious, concentrated expressions.

- What are they doing?

  We are discussing a difficult case. A thick file is open on the coffee table between us. Sue is pointing to something in the file. Several reference books are also an the table. Some are open.

- How are they dressed?

  I am wearing my usual T-shirt and black jeans. Paul has a green shirt and blue tie that somehow work for him. Sue looks very professional in a dark blue suit, she's taken her jacket off and it can be seen over the back of her chair. Her white shirt looks clean and crisp.

- What are they holding in their hands?

Sue points at the file as Paul and I hold mugs of coffee. I've got a pen in my other hand prepared to write in a notepad on my lap.

- What's in the background?

Filing cabinets; photocopier; flip-chart; and desks are behind us. The desks are mostly piled with files and paper. Only one is neat without clutter. Some plants struggle to survive in the artificial light.

- Is it day or night?

It's daytime but getting dark outside. The light is bright and artificial.

- What single detail is most interesting?

The one tidy desk has a rather large model of the Eiffel Tower on it.

- There is one thing in this photo that doesn't belong. What is it?

Among the textbooks on the table is a diet book that belongs to me.

Exercise 34

Storytelling

Purpose

In this affirming exercise, participants work in pairs, encouraging sharing, group cohesion, and evaluation from another's perspective. The exercise is based on trust and participants need to feel safe with each other.

Method

In pairs of listener and speaker, group members tell a partner about their favourite or least favourite place for a carefully timed two minutes. (The facilitator must serve as time-keeper.) The listener can take notes but will not interrupt the speaker during this time. During the next two minutes, the listener can ask questions of the speaker and continue noting down his or her responses. Now the roles are reversed. After the second person tells their story, the writing begins.

The listener writes up the speaker's tale, in the first person, as if they were the speaker.

Many topics can be used as the basis for this storytelling exercise. Other possibilities might include: **'The time we all co-operated, or couldn't co-operate'**; **'The time I had a conflict at work'**; **'The time I felt real satisfaction with my job'**.

8 minutes for storytelling.
10 minutes for writing.

Example

Topic: **'The time we all co-operated'**

Teamwork is important but our work is so scattered that I often don't even see many of my colleagues, let alone work with them. I often feel I'm alone in my work with intractable problems. There was a time, though, when we all decided to do something about it.

At a team meeting we were all moaning about how reactive

our work was. 'We can't see the wood for the trees', said someone. Then an idea arose, I can't say who thought of it, it was just there. A project we could all work on that might make a difference.

I was amazed at the response. People who were usually first out of meetings held back with the rest of us to plan the project. We all felt positive and ideas flowed like Greek wine. We divided ourselves into teams, each with a task and a deadline for reporting back. We didn't have to be told what to do. Everyone was so enthused it was catching. Even the most cynical of us got carried away. Time could be a problem but we all agreed to do some of the work in our own time.

There was a buzz around the office for weeks as people came in early or left late discussing the project. I felt excited about work again. The project itself was interesting but it was the way we all were involved, interested and together that really generated excitement.

Time and events have taken their toll and we're back to the day-to-day grind. The difference is that I know things can get better.

Exercise 35

Eight lines

Purpose

By asking participants to do this unusual exercise, which requires thinking about two different things at once, you often get fresh ideas and surprising responses. This is a good exercise to finish off with because it is fun, the results are usually exciting, and by the end of a workshop, participants ought to be unfazed by crazy exercises.

Method

Ask participants to write an eight-line unrhyming poem on a topic relevant to the workshop. Sounds simple enough, but there's a complication coming.

In a recent workshop I gave in Newcastle, on 'The contributions older people can make to society', I asked participants, who were all older people themselves, to write a poem on the theme, 'I won't be a burden'. The complication was that they were asked to write these eight lines on the given theme, while mentioning **a weather condition** in each line. I got groans and complains; people said, '*This would have been easy if you had just asked us to write about being a burden.*' Of course, it would have. But they all did the exercise and the results, because the writers were forced to think in a new, admittedly restrictive and peculiar way, were startling. The results were surprising especially for the use of simile and metaphor: the writers were forced to compare themselves, their emotions, conditions, hopes and fears to other things.

The complication can be any subject that provides a lot of related words (e.g. **food and drink, animals, articles of furniture, plants and flowers, vehicles, sounds**).

Read around.

10 minutes.

Variations

Write an eight-line unrhyming poem on a given theme by beginning each line with, **'I wish ...'** (In a second draft participants can experiment with rewriting by deleting this phrase and adding or subtracting any other words to make the poem work.)

Write an eight-line unrhyming poem on a given theme with the beginning of each line alternating between **Once ...** and **Now ...**

Write an eight-line unrhyming poem on a given theme making each line **a lie**.

Example

Theme: **'I won't be a burden'**

Complication: **'A weather condition must be mentioned in each line'**

If my mind starts to fog as I grow old, I won't be a burden.
I'll freeze in my home.
Not letting you know till a thaw sets in.
I'll keep dry in the rain, and cool in the sun.
I'll bear the cutting wind.
Some fine day, I'll phone.
Although my thundering voice has deserted me.
In the autumn sun, I might still flower.

PART 3

Workshops

A typical workshop

This workshop was held in Newcastle upon Tyne on September 11 1998, from 9.30am to 12.30pm. The aim was to bring together people who worked in social services and who were in the prime of their professional lives to express feelings about older people and their contribution to society. I also planned to ask them to project themselves into old age, to imagine what that would be like, and to record what their hopes for themselves at that time of life would be. There were 16 people present.

9.30 We began on time with an ice-breaking Object Riddle (see Exercise 1). I had prepared the envelope to include objects traditionally associated with old age, such as bus pass, pension book, grey hair, bifocals.

I introduced the exercise. As this was the first exercise, and there were a lot of apprehensive people who had never done any creative writing before, I gave everyone a hand-out, an already-prepared example of a riddle, as well as simple printed instructions. I believe this made the task less daunting. What was required was very specific, very concrete. (At the beginning of a workshop, a hand-out gives people a sense of security. After a group gains writing confidence, you can do without hand-outs.)

I carefully explained the hand-out, reading it out. The participants had 5 minutes' writing time.

As we near the time limit, I usually look around and see how many people are still writing, how many have put their pens down. It is important to stop once you see most people have finished even though they might have done so in less than the time required, so as to avoid lengthy or polished responses. This group took slightly less than 5 minutes.

We read around the responses and guessed the objects.

The way I organise reading aloud is to start with a different group member for each exercise and go around the table clockwise. This gives a kind of inevitability to each reading, rather than a randomness. (Participants can see it coming.) As there were 16 people in this workshop the read-around took a bit of time. (For a short piece of writing, I usually figure on a minute per person.)

The whole exercise took 25 minutes.

9.55 The second exercise, Photographs (see Exercise 33) was introduced. I asked group members to imagine that they were looking at a photo of themselves in 20 years' time. I asked the various questions included in this exercise, one by one, and waited while they answered in a sentence or two of prose, watching for them to finish. (About 2 minutes per question.)

I could have handed out the list of questions and asked them to use them as writing notes, but I felt that this exercise, because it was risky and required an emotional honesty, needed to be guided. The more risky the content, the more guided the directions and method should be. There were ten questions, so it took 20 minutes to do this exercise. Because of the nature of the questions, and the specific method, group members were able to read around immediately without going over their pieces. (It is always good to avoid too much polishing in these workshops.) The responses to each sentence, when read together sounded like continuous prose. The reading around took 20 minutes.

Although I had not asked them specifically to evaluate issues surrounding ageing in our society, the group produced work which strongly indicated their attitudes. There were so many issues that came up in this exercise we could have stopped there and had many fruitful discussions. We didn't do this because a specific aim of this workshop was to produce writing that could be used on posters, banners and in pamphlets at a forthcoming event on older people and their contribution to society. (The group was aware that the writing they produced might be used in this way.)

This exercise took 40 minutes.

10.35 The third exercise was, Remembering the Present (see Exercise 12). I thought this exercise was particularly apt for the aims of this workshop, because I was asking people to view their current concerns, from a distance of years, as if they themselves were elderly. The three line response also would produce short bits of writing we could use for our forthcoming event.

The key words I gave the group were: I remember . . . My desk, A particular shop, A conflict, A child, A letter, An insight, An illness, A friend.

The first two key words – My desk, A particular shop – were purposefully less emotionally charged than later words.

After the group recorded their three-line response to the first word, we read around to make sure everyone was doing the exercise correctly. (Although some of the exercises in this workbook are simply excuses to get people writing, many depend on following the rules exactly.) After hearing these first responses, I advised the group to try to write in shorter sentences as they were attempting to cram too much into their three sentences. Their sentences sounded more like paragraphs. We talked about saying less and hinting at more, or using the three sentences available to play with rhythm and tone, by making one or two sentences long and the third, or last sentence, short and stark.

We resumed the exercise, working through all the key words. The exercise took 20 minutes to complete.

I asked group members to choose their favourite response. The first person to read, read only their favourite (My Desk, for instance). Then when we went around the room, everyone else read their response to the same key word.

The results were poignant, funny and often quite emotional. Some of the emotional responses to this exercise caused tears. While a bit distressing, it gave the group (largely people who didn't know each other before, but worked in the same field) the opportunity to support one another. Which they did.

10.55 We continued reading out, but it was taking a long time, and had been very emotional. I decided we needed to break, after we heard everyone's response to six of the eight key words.

Although I realised some of the work had not yet been read and could not be shared if we moved on, I felt this was a compromise I had to make.

In general it is important to try to hear everyone's response to an exercise and never leave any participant without time to read. In this particular exercise, however, everyone had responded by reading some of what they'd written, so while not ideal, I figured it was all right to move on.

11.30 Coffee and tea break.

Even without highly emotional responses, creative writing is intense. Participants need breaks. In general, it might prove difficult to ask people to do any more than four exercises in a half-day workshop, six for a whole day.

11:45 When we returned to writing we attempted Role Models (see Exercise 26). This was fairly straightforward and took ten minutes' writing time, 15 minutes' reading time.

We ended the workshop with an Acrostic (see Exercise 19) turning the name of our role model into an acrostic poem. This took 5 minutes plus to complete. (By now people were writing with much more ease and confidence.) The exercise was read out in 15 minutes.

It's often good to end with something snappy that results in a short, finished piece of writing like an acrostic.

There was more I wanted to do. As usually I had overplanned. We ended at 12.30 exactly. As well as retrieving valuable information for our event, I heard several participants comment on how much they enjoyed the workshop. 'This is the first thing I've done for myself in a while,' someone said. A challenge had been met, and more. Participants seemed to feel a sense of personal fulfilment.

How to put a session together

Tailoring exercises for particular groups and issues means both responsibility and freedom for facilitator. When planning the session it is important to have an idea of the kind of data you want to generate. You should also make some judgement about the make-up of the group.

You can now begin to select exercises that will address your aims for the session. Start with ice-breakers and easier exercises. You can progress to whatever level of difficulty you feel the group can cope with.

When you have selected the exercises you should think about tailoring them to the needs of your session. Almost all of the exercises can be adapted to your needs. I have suggested ways to adapt some of them. Look at my suggestions; see how it is done; think about what information you want; use your imagination.

Your session should be balanced in terms of having an ascending level of difficulty, a range of writing techniques and a balance between prose and poetry. You should aim for the session to be fun, stimulating, exciting and demanding.

Ground rules for facilitators

Creative writing can be a liberating and democratic format for exploring issues, processes and problems. Facilitating a creative-writing workshop involves asking participants to do unfamiliar things that may expose very personal and perhaps painful aspects of their working and/or personal life. As a facilitator you must take responsibility for ensuring that the environment is physically and emotionally safe for risk-taking. The following ground rules will help you develop a trusting and supportive session:

- Share aims with participants, share process.
- Clearly state the rules of each exercise. The boundaries are enablers so they need to be enforced.
- Build intensity and difficulty. Start with easy exercises.
- When an exercise has various components or parts, don't give all the directions out at once. Let participants experience the exercise bit by bit without knowing what's coming next.
- Make the atmosphere safe for sharing and risk-taking.
- Establish an order for reading out. Establish time boundaries.
- Using guidelines offered, plan the number of participants, seating arrangements, hand-outs (prepared examples of published or workshop-produced writing as permission/guidance for participants).
- Make sure standards and expectations are reasonable, emphasise experience, fun.
- Where appropriate, initiate group discussion around issues that arise.
- Be aware of what is going on in terms of group processes. The process is very experiential, e.g. bonding.
- Encourage, be positive, remind participants that they are doing something new, give them a sense of achievement.

- If possible, try to give some feedback on each piece of writing that is read out. Notice similarities and differences to the other pieces of writing that have been read, ask the writer questions about the writing or the process, explore the effect of the piece. Does this piece lend itself to general discussion?

Common problems

Problem

Some participants can think what they are doing is silly, impractical, cannot see the point.

Solution

Provide motivation. Clearly state why they are doing these exercises. Emphasise that these techniques have been successfully used elsewhere. Take it seriously yourself.

Problem

Some participants will not be able to do particular exercises.

Solution

At the beginning of the workshop, explain that all the exercises are different. Experiencing problems with a particular exercise does not necessarily mean having problems with all the exercises. If a person cannot do an exercise then it doesn't matter, although everyone needs to try to do something.

Start with easier, more accessible exercises, build to more difficult ones.

Get the timing right. Various times are suggested for the given exercises. More time does not necessarily mean an exercise will be easier to do. Often the opposite is true.

Make sure the participants are not expecting too much of themselves. Emphasise the idea that they are scribbling, improvising, getting thoughts down, rather than producing polished writing. In the time allotted it would be impossible to produce a polished piece, anyway. Time restrictions give the writer freedom to play rather than polish.

Ask why a particular exercise has been difficult. The reasons behind this can be as important for evaluation purposes as information from an exercise easily done.

Problem

Some people will not read out loud.

Solution

It is OK not to read a particular piece, but it would be good to try to read something, to have one's voice heard.

Ask if it is OK for someone else to read the piece (perhaps the facilitator).

Give positive feedback; check that the atmosphere is safe.

Problem

People are getting tired.

Solution

Remind participants that this is more difficult and demanding than it seems.

Participants need breaks.

There's often a temptation to try too much in one session. Restrict your aims.

Think about scheduling further sessions rather than trying to cram too much into this one. I would normally prepare about four exercises for a half-day workshop; six exercises for a full day.

Vary the pace with discussion. Keep a simpler exercise in reserve – for example, a more light-hearted ice-breaker can be used in the middle of the session.

Problem

Some people aren't following directions.

Solution

Although you're aiming for a safe, relaxed atmosphere, you must stress that following the guidelines and directions is crucial. Asking participants to do unusual things within strict guidelines and time limits is the key. Participants may need a lot of structure to feel confident enough to try the exercises. Writing becomes a matter of following a pattern or a recipe, rather than a risky artistic involvement with 'the Muse.'

How to use the information you've generated

- Use it to create new questions as well as providing answers.
- Use the information in conjunction with other research methods to build up a picture of layers of reality.
- Describe how the sessions affected the participants and yourself. Not only is what happens in the workshop important, but *how* it happens. Be aware of changing group processes: this is an important outcome.

Further reading

Angela Everitt and Pauline Hardiker's book, *Evaluating for Good Practice*, published by Macmillan, discusses subjective evaluation in relation to social welfare. I strongly recommend that anyone interested in the subject should read it. The authors look at the purposes of evaluation and conclude that it should aim to identify and encourage good practice. Everitt and Hardiker stress the need for making judgements about practice as part of the process of improving the quality of practice.

Creative writing, as an evaluative tool, can provide some of the information necessary for making such judgements. The democratic nature of creative writing, its emphasis on the individual's viewpoint and the fact that everyone can tell a story, all make creative writing an exciting and useful medium for the evaluation of social processes.